The Wit
of Women

The Toast is:
　　　　'The Ladies'

The Wit of Women

Compiled by

Lore and Maurice Cowan

Aurora Publishers Incorporated
NASHVILLE/LONDON

FIRST PUBLISHED 1969
LESLIE FREWIN PUBLISHERS LIMITED
LONDON, ENGLAND

COPYRIGHT © 1970 BY
AURORA PUBLISHERS INCORPORATED
NASHVILLE, TENNESSEE 37219
LIBRARY OF CONGRESS CATALOG CARD NUMBER: 78-125582
STANDARD BOOK NUMBER: 87695-035-7
MANUFACTURED IN THE UNITED STATES OF AMERICA

CONTENTS

Introduction	7
From Eve Onwards	9
The Dames	70
Anonymous	78
Love and Marriage	80
Mistresses and Courtesans	93
Men	105
Politics	119
Food	128
Beauty and Fashion	134
Stage and Screen	143
Acknowledgments	168
Index	171

Introduction

SINCE THIS IS the first book exclusively devoted to the wit of women, I feel that it merits an introduction by a woman.

From the dawn of civilisation, man has boasted of his superiority over woman, and through the ages he has always adopted a condescending pat-on-the-head attitude towards her.

From biblical times to the present day, man has praised woman for her beauty and her virtue, condemned her for her frailty and her fickleness, decided she was 'uncertain, coy and hard to please', and in the same breath labelled her a 'ministering angel'.

Of wit, never a word.

True, one man, Lord Chesterfield, grudgingly admitted that sometimes woman had wit, but immediately regretted this by declaring that a man of sense only trifles with women, plays with them, humours and flatters them, but never consults them on serious matters.

Some of the blame for this must be attributed to ourselves for, as Nobel prizewinner Pearl Buck says, we women too easily accept the idea of man's superiority, if not actually, then in order to curry favour with men, who imagine it easier to live with inferiors than with equals.

One reason man gave – and still gives – for his alleged

superiority, is that woman lacks wit. This book is a complete refutation of this false assertion.

For centuries it was considered reprehensible in women to be witty, but they came into their own, particularly in France, in the 18th and 19th centuries, when they proved themselves as witty as the men.

Naturally, man was – and still is – an excellent target. With unerring aim his façade of superiority has been shattered.

Speak to any woman writer, and you see the twinkle in her eye when she scores a hit on man.

While it is impossible to do complete justice to the wit of contemporary women in this volume, we considered it high time that the notable and quotable women journalists should be given just due.

Remembering that Oscar Wilde said 'Never trust a woman who tells her real age', I have decided that we should omit the birth date of our living contributors, and so avoid any recriminations.

From conversations I have had, I learn that there is a general desire for a definition of the word WIT, but I am not imprudent enough to rush in where so many eminent people have feared to tread.

I leave the last word to Margaret, Duchess of Newcastle (1625–1673): 'Wit is like the Elixir that keeps Nature always fresh and young'.

Lore Cowan

I blush with shame at man's inhumanity to woman, but I agree with every word my wife has written.

I console myself with the fact that it was a man who said that woman 'made brutes men, and men divine'.

Maurice Cowan

From Eve Onwards

When God asked Eve, the 'mother of all living', why she had eaten the fruit of the forbidden tree of the knowledge of good and evil, she had the wit to reply:

'The serpent beguiled me', the classic excuse of women since the Creation.

Polly Adler

Title of her autobiography – *A House is not a Home*.

It's not a college degree that makes a writer. The great thing is to have a story to tell.

Too many cooks spoil the brothel.

After girl gets boy, why should a two-buck marriage licence entitle her to turn off all that charm she turned on during courtship?

Your heart often knows things before your mind does.

*   *   *

Margot Asquith (1864-1945)

All the faults of the age come from Christianity and journalism.

Truthfulness with me is hardly a virtue. I cannot discriminate between truths that need and those that need not to be told.

One of my complaints about the shortness of life is that there is not enough time to feel pity and love for enough people.

Those who have neither the candour, generosity, or humbleness, to say that they are wrong are not worth loving.

Summing up her life at one period –

A lot of love-making and a little abuse; a little fame and more abuse; a real man and great happiness; the love of children and seventh heaven; an early death and a crowded memorial service.

What a pity when Christopher Columbus discovered America that he ever mentioned it.

Rumour is untraceable, incalculable, and infectious. It shapes public men in the opinion of ignorant people, but is seldom right.

I have always longed to have the qualities that I do not possess, but I have not got *all* the defects that I am accused of.

If the temper of your mind gets interwoven with your convictions, you lose in heat what you might gain by reason.

The question of sex dominates the destinies of half mankind. How wearisome too much dilation upon it can become.

Beds today play an important part both in fiction and on the stage.

The copy books should have written 'Vanity is the root of all evil', not 'Money'.

Flattery is like icing on a cake. You can never guess whether the foundation of it is seed, sponge, or sultana.

On religion –

You might as well try and find a fox in an omnibus, as find God by your reason.

There is nothing more perplexing in life than to know at what point you should surrender your intellect to your faith.

*   *   *

Lady Nancy Astor (1879-1964)

Ever since Eve ate the apple we are up against generations and generations of prejudice – it was not simply because it was good for food or pleasant to the eyes: it was from a tree whose fruit would make one wise——

The first time Adam had a chance he laid the blame on woman.

A fool without fear is sometimes wiser than an angel with fear.

It isn't common man who is important. It's the uncommon man.

My vigour, vitality, and cheek repel me. I am the kind of woman I would run away from.

On her 80th birthday –

Years ago, I thought old age would be dreadful, because I should not be able to do things I would want to do. Now I find there is nothing I want to do after all.

*   *   *

Madame Aubernon

Advice to a young matron who wanted to run a 'salon' –

Don't try! You have too luscious a bosom to keep the conversation general.

Commenting on her husband who left her after a few years –

My husband and I will soon be celebrating our golden anniversary of cloudless separation.

Caught reading Ibsen by a friend –

Don't disturb me! I'm in the midst of acquiring a Norwegian soul!

* * *

Jane Austen (1775-1817)

One man's way may be as good as another's, but we all like our own best.

In nine cases out of ten, a woman had better show more affection than she feels.

It is better to know as little as possible of the defects of the person with whom you are to pass your life.

A woman, especially if she have the misfortune of knowing anything, should conceal it as well as she can.

History tells me nothing that does not either vex or weary me; the men are all so good for nothing, and hardly any women at all.

* * *

Lady Aylesbury

Always be nice to girls; you never know who they will become.

* * *

Lady Isobel Barnett

I don't want to be a slave to anything, even fame.

I would rather be a dumb blonde than an egghead.

Anatomically speaking, a bust is here today and gone tomorrow.

Life belongs to the pretty woman.

* * *

Marie Bashkirtseff (1860-1884)

There are musicians who have only a few notes, and painters who have but few colours.

To sell dear is very good, for there has never been really brilliant glory without gold.

* * *

Duchess of Bedford

I used to lead a leisurely life, the life of a duchess, until I married and became a duchess. It's all work, work, work.

*   *   *

Aphra Behn (1640-1689)

Money speaks sense in a language all nations understand.

He that will live in this world must be endowed with the three rare qualities of dissimulation, equivocation, and mental reservation.

Come away; poverty's catching.

*   *   *

Charlotte Bingham

No wearer of a liberty bodice has ever been famed for her promiscuity, and the rarity nowadays of both liberty bodices and virgins is undeniable.

A twenty-five-year-old virgin is like the man who was set upon by thieves: everyone passes by.

Elizabeth I was a great example to working virgins. Not only had she been good at her job, but she was clever enough to know that, while love was all very well, once

Leicester bounced her she'd never keep the same grip on things. So she strung along, and by and large did very well for herself.

Giving away a fortune is taking Christianity too far.

* * *

Madeleine Bingham (Lady Clanmorris)

There is still a feeling about that peers (and peeresses) are symbolic of all that is rotten in the state of this country.

When it comes down to it, it is only money that commands respect. But, if you are a Beatle, to live modestly is a virtue; if you are a lord, it invites contempt.

Modern sexual theories, carried to their logical extreme, would seem to prove that the ladies of the town are the best-adjusted women in London – a premise I am reluctant to accept.

* * *

Countess of Blessington (1789-1849)

A profound knowledge of life is the least enviable of all species of knowledge, because it can only be acquired by trials that make us regret the loss of our ignorance.

When we find that we are not liked, we assert that we are not understood; when probably the dislike we have excited proceeds from our being too fully comprehended.

Happiness, like youth and health, is rarely appreciated until it is past.

Society punishes not the vices of its members, but their detection.

Happiness consists not in having much, but in being content with little.

Bores: people who talk of themselves when you are thinking only of yourself.

Friends are the thermometers by which we may judge the temperature of our fortunes.

Pleasure is like a cordial – a little of it is not injurious, but too much destroys.

Virtue, like a dowerless beauty, has more admirers than followers.

The vices of the rich and great are mistaken for errors, and those of the poor and lonely for crimes.

Truth and physic, two unpalatable things, are never well received, though administered with good intention.

Scandal is the offspring of envy and malice – nursed by society, and cultivated by disappointment.

There are no persons as capable of stooping so low as those who desire to rise in the world.

The rich suffer from want of appetite, the poor from excess.

No dust affects the eyes so much as gold dust.

Sorrow is to youth what experience is to maternity.

Kings never hear the voice of truth until they are dethroned, nor beauties until they have abdicated their charms.

It is usually the most conceited people who take offence at the affection of others.

Friends, like wine, require to be kept before use.

Prejudices are the chains forged by ignorance to keep men apart.

Fatality is another name for misconduct.

Praise is the only gift for which people are really grateful.

The most certain art of pleasing people with us is to make them pleased with themselves.

People are seldom tired of the world until the world is tired of them.

They who weep over errors, were not formed for crimes.

Wit lives in the present, but genius survives in the future.

There is no cosmetic for beauty like happiness.

Catherine I of Russia was called the mother of her people; but Catherine II might, with nearly equal justice, be named the *wife*.

* * *

Naomi Bliven

Behind almost every woman you ever heard of stands a man who let her down.

Except for Queen Victoria, happy matrons have no history.

* * *

Anne Boleyn (1507-1536)

I am the first Queen of England to go to the scaffold – a doubtful distinction. I shall be a saint in heaven. I will be easily nicknamed 'Anne *sans-tête*'.

* * *

Phyllis Bottome (1884-1963)

Nothing ever really sets human nature free, but self-control.

* * *

Nancy Boyd (1892-1950)

I like Americans.
They are not grown up yet. They still believe in Santa
                                                  Claus. . . .
I like Americans.
They smoke with their meals. . . .
I like Americans.
They are so ridiculous.
They are always risking their lives to save a minute.

The Italians are nice.
But they are not so nice as the Americans.
They have been told that they live in a warm climate,
And they refuse to heat their houses.
They are forever sobbing Puccini.
They no longer have lions about to prey on Christian flesh.
But they have more than a sufficient supply of certain
                                          smaller carnivora.
And if you walk in the street alone, somebody pinches
                                                      you.

He was a man of parts, but badly assembled.

The Englishman fox-trots as he fox-hunts, with all his being, through thickets, through ditches, over hedges, through chiffons, through waiters, over saxophones, to the victorious finish: and who goes home depends on how many the ambulance will accommodate.

* * *

Charlotte Brontë (1816-1855)

Life appears to me too short to be spent in nursing animosity or registering wrongs.

I can be on my guard against my enemies, but God deliver me from my friends.

*   *   *

Elizabeth Barrett Browning (1806-1861)

If we tried to sink the past beneath our feet, be sure the future would not stand it.

Since when was genius found respectable?

*   *   *

Pearl Buck

We send missionaries to China so the Chinese can get into heaven, but we won't let them into our country.

Women in America too easily accept the idea of their inferiority to men – if not actually, then in order to curry favour with men, who imagine it easier to live with inferiors than with equals.

The old bogey of the loss of sex or sex charm through doing a particular job in the world is nothing but nonsense, repeated once more by some individual for his own self-defence for something or other.

Sex is exciting only when it is a subtle and pervasive part of the relationship between men and women, varying in its form from adolescence to old age, and it dies only with death if it is properly nourished in life.

* * *

Catherine the Great (1729-1796)

Study mankind. Learn to use men without surrendering to them. Have confidence in those who, if necessary, are courageous enough to contradict you.

First health, then wealth, then pleasure, and do not owe anything to anybody.

I never answer Jeremiahs.

Don't worry about things you cannot alter.

* * *

Queen Charlotte (1744-1818)

I am always quarrelling with time! It is so short to do something and so long to do nothing.

* * *

Ilka Chase

Art, we are told, is a criterion of one's taste. How humiliating, should our taste turn out to be bad. Rather as though we were caught stark naked with a poor figure.

Let a man beware of loving his country too much; let him be sure that his devotion to his native land does not imply hatred of every other.

America's best buy for a nickel (when it was a nickel) is a telephone call to the right man.

George Moore unexpectedly pinched my behind. I felt rather honoured that my behind should have drawn the attention of the great master of English prose.

* * *

Christina of Sweden (1626-1689)

Having abdicated the throne of Sweden, she turned her life into a tragi-comedy. She was nicknamed the 'Queen of Sodom'.

To live and to die beautifully is the science of sciences.

To believe all is weakness; to believe nothing is stupidity.

* * *

Agatha Christie

On 'Laughter in Court' –

If that's not caused by one of the Judge's remarks, you'll find he'll soon threaten to have the Court cleared.

Any woman can fool a man if she wants to and if he's in love with her.

* * *

Anne of Cleves (1515-1557)

Asked by her Lady-in-waiting if she is still a maid –

How can I be a maid and sleep every night with the King? When he comes to bed he kisses me, takes me by the hand and bids me 'Goodnight, sweetheart', and in the morning, he kisses me and bids me 'Farewell darling!' Is not this enough?

* * *

Colette (1873-1954)

When a woman in love reaches a certain age, though her heart may cease to sing, her eyes remain veiled with gratitude.

A woman who remains a woman remains a complete being.

It is prudent to pour the oil of delicate politeness upon the machinery of friendship.

Mental freedom, taken and used in good society, is an enchantment.

With jealousy, one has no time to be bored, and hardly time to grow old.

Jealousy is the only evil we endure without becoming accustomed to it.

Time rewards fair opponents.

*   *   *

Lady Diana Cooper

In astrology there is room for precaution and obstruction; the disaster is not inevitable. One can dodge the stars in their courses.

Age wins and one must learn to grow old.

*   *   *

Fleur Cowles

The seating plan for the very formal annual United Nations Security Council dinner in New York City once placed editor-author, Fleur Cowles, next to a stranger, the Ambassador of a colonial power in Africa. It was, in fact, a country which she had only recently visited, where she narrowly avoided arrest for having unwittingly broken the law by seeing persons not popular with the Government. As the Ambassador helped her into her chair, he curtly remarked –

'I have just had a full report on every biased and inaccurate and unfriendly remark you have recently made about my country.'

'How very interesting,' Fleur Cowles replied. 'You must be the Ambassador from . . . You may now have the whole dinner for your rebuttal.'

* * *

Hannah Cowley (1743-1809)

What is a woman? Only one of Nature's agreeable blunders.

Love taken up late in life has a bad effect on the temper.

Vanity, like murder, will out.

* * *

Mrs Edmund Craster (d 1874)

> The Centipede was happy quite,
> Until the Toad in fun
> Said 'Pray which leg goes after which?'
> And worked her mind to such a pitch,
> She lay distracted in the ditch
> Considering how to run.

* * *

Clemence Dane (1888-1965)

Make us laugh and you can pick all pockets.

*   *   *

Geneviève Antoine Dariaux

Admiration is as indispensable to life as oxygen.

Definition of an Angel –

'Mary, be an angel and get me my shirt!'
'Mother, be an angel and sew on this button for me!'
If you have been an angel all day long, when evening comes you'll find that you are dead on your feet, but you haven't yet grown wings.

Arrogance pays off only in history books.

Cinderella's slipper has been replaced by the X brassière.

Habit –

>   is the chloroform of love.
>   is the cement that unites married couples.
>   is getting stuck in the mud of daily routine.
>   is the fog that masks the most beautiful scenery.
>   is the end of everything.

In business, as in love, exaggerated zeal is very tiring.

We no longer live yesterday, and we haven't yet lived tomorrow, so the only thing that counts is today.

A stranger loses half his charm the day he is no longer a stranger.

* * *

Lady Dartmouth

Shopping can be fun. It can be an emotional outlet. Women go shopping to buy friendship and flattery from the assistant. For some women, shopping is a sex compensation. So the shop must seduce the customer.

English women have a habit of letting themselves go after thirty. They seem to think, once they are married, they can give up trying. I would make-up just the same if I were on a desert island.

Falling in love with the boss is the cardinal sin in the office. A girl must look after her boss – be a friend, public relations officer, colleague, and nanny – but never love him. Nothing is more boring or irritating to his friends and colleagues than an adoring and possessive secretary.

Advice on how to be the perfect secretary can be summed up in three words – use your loaf.

* * *

Marquise du Defand (1697-1780)

Women are too imaginative to have much power of reasoning.

* * *

Madame Deshoulières (1634-1694)

No one is content with his fortune, nor discontent with his intellect.

We begin by being fools, and end by becoming knaves.

* * *

Emily Dickinson (1830-1886)

> Success is counted sweetest
> By those who ne'er succeed.

> How dreary to be somebody!
> How public like a frog,
> To tell your name the livelong day
> To an admiring hog!

> Faith is a fine invention
> For gentlemen who see;
> But microscopes are prudent
> In an emergency!

* * *

Magaret Drabble

Nothing succeeds, they say, like success, and certainly nothing fails like failure.

* * *

Nell Dunn

Commenting on her forthright play UP THE JUNCTION –

If I wrote a play about my own life people would be far more shocked. I feel sex is a good thing. It makes people better people, and I think that desiring and loving, and even having people, is the best thing life has to offer.

I'm glad that I'm a woman because women can get away with a lot. They don't need to know facts, and can be more indefinite. Having children is much the best thing in life.

I'm glad I'm a woman because I don't have to worry about getting men pregnant.

* * *

Maria Edgeworth (1767-1849)

Some people talk of morality, and some of religion, but give me a little snug property.

Come when you're called;
And do as you're bid;
Shut the door after you;
And you'll never be chid.

*   *   *

Anne Edwards

Advice to girls –

No more paying your whack, going fifty-fifty when he takes you out. If there's no equality in pay, why should there be equality in paying out – Play it right and you'll even have them getting up to offer you their seat in a train.

*   *   *

George Eliot (1819-1880)

Friendship begins with liking or gratitude – roots that can be pulled up.

She is like the rest of women – thinks two and two'll come to five, if she cries and bothers enough about it.

The happiest women, like the happiest nations, have no history.

We are all apt to believe what the world believes about us.

A fool or idiot is one who expects things to happen that never can happen.

Among all forms of mistake, prophecy is the most gratuitous.

Correct English is the slang of prigs.

* * *

'Elizabeth' (Lady Russell) (1886-1941)

Home after all is the best place when life begins to wobble.

I think nothing great was done by anyone who wasted time peering about among his faults.

* * *

Queen Elizabeth I (1533-1603)

Her favourite maxim –

Video et taceo (I see and am silent).

Do not tell secrets to those whose faith and silence you have not already tested.

There is no marvel in a woman learning to speak, but there would be in teaching her to hold her tongue.

I do not keep a dog and bark myself.

To a lady of Queen Mary's household who had been cruel to Elizabeth –

Fear not, we are of the nature of the lion, and cannot descend to the destruction of mice and such small beasts.

Our common adage we have in England is a very good one: when one fears that an evil is coming, the sooner it arrives, the better.

Although I may not be a lioness, I am a lion's cub, and inherit many of his qualities.

* * *

Lady Anne Fanshawe (1625-1680)

Advice to her son –

Endeavour to be innocent as a dove, but as wise as a serpent.

* * *

Edna Ferber (1887-1968)

Being an old maid is like death by drowning, a really delightful sensation after you cease to struggle.

A woman can look both moral and exciting – if she also looks as if it was quite a struggle.

Life can't defeat a writer who is in love with writing, for life itself is a writer's lover until death.

* * *

THE WIT OF WOMEN

Joan Fleming

Concerning writing about nasty things like murder –

I am not nice and I am certainly not a lady. I am from Lancashire and they don't breed ladies there.

* * *

Penelope Gilliatt

On the dullness of Sunday –

Sunday should be abolished except between consenting adults in private.

Quoting a man who had twins at seventy-eight –

The chap said to me once, when we were talking about this: 'Some do, some don't. Some can, some can't. I'm a "can" *and* "do".'

A temperament born of two gins below par.

A scientist on woman –

The worst fact about woman is that she cries so easily. There's a vicious trick of the ducts for you. One blow in the places she minds about, loyalty, keeping things going, all that, and the waterworks start and she's cooked her own goose, for there's not a man who can forgive a woman for crying.

* * *

Elinor Glyn (1864-1943)

There are three things a woman ought to look – straight as a dart, supple as a snake, and proud as a tiger lily.

Try to remember to accept Fate without noise.

Priests, and custom, and convention, have robbed the world of much joy.

* * *

Virginia Graham

No woman need feel the smallest twinge of shame at being as stupid as an egg. Plain women should know just a little more than pretty ones, and downright ugly ones just a bit more still; but no woman, whatever her physiognomy, should know more than a man. That is, if she wants to be loved by him.

Concerning the Ballet –

The only really important thing to remember is that Pavlova was a Swan, and that she was it for about thirty years.

Grace is a virtue which a lady would be wise to hold on to. Let it go for a moment and she becomes a woman, which, as any woman will tell you, is a very depressing thing to be.

On Cocktail Parties –

It is not done to let anybody be too happy. The moment two people seem to be enjoying one another's company, a good hostess introduces a third element or removes the first.

A lady who knows only her husband at a cocktail party needn't be too depressed. Many husbands and wives have had extraordinarily interesting conversations in such circumstances.

* * *

Texas Guinan

Success has killed more men than bullets.

* * *

Sonja Henie

She has accumulated enough jewellery in ten years to tip the scales at her weight of 7 st 5 lbs –

They take people's mind off your wrinkles.

* * *

Patricia Highsmith

It's true I understand nuts, kinky, kooky people. I don't understand ordinary people. . . . I have a lurking liking for those who flaunt the law, which I realise is despicable of me. . . . Women tend to be good at inventing ingenious plots. They do it all the time.

* * *

Hedda Hopper (1890-1966)

Having only friends would be dull anyway – like eating eggs without salt.
I wasn't allowed to speak while my husband was alive, and since he's gone no one has been able to shut me up.

Behind a name in lights you'll find a hundred helping hands.

* * *

Julia Ward Howe (1819-1910)

Asked, when old, whether it wasn't hard to grow old –

I don't find it so. The deeper I drink the cup, the sweeter it tastes – all the sugar's at the bottom.

* * *

Fannie Hurst (1889-1968)

When the mind's eye turns inward, it blazes upon the dearly beloved image of oneself.

One of the compensations of maturity is to be able to observe the lives of your contemporaries in the round, so to speak.

Women, on the whole, do not seem to fancy their sex. Their indictments are: Women are feline. Gossipy. Petty. Deadly competitive.

'Little people' is a man-coined phrase. I doubt if we were meant to be graded as eggs.

* * *

Margery Hurst

If she wants to get to the top, a woman must be prepared to work ninety per cent harder than a man.

For girls aiming at the top –

Find the right field and stick to it.

You can destroy somebody completely if you hammer them with negative criticism.

Any girl who takes pride in her appearance is bound to be a good worker.

The perfect secretary anticipates her boss's demands and wishes, worries about his welfare. She never takes part in his life outside the office.

The hand that rocks the cradle may not rule the world, but it certainly makes it a better place.

A woman's world is much more than babies and recipes.

* * *

Catherine Hyde (1700-1777)

When Horace Walpole drank to her, wishing that she might live to grow ugly, she replied –

I hope, then, you will keep your taste for antiquities.

* * *

Angela Ince

Rights are all very well, but as a woman I'd rather have privileges – above all, the blessed privilege of frailty: 'Let me carry that heavy old matchbox for you, dearest', husbands used to murmur to pregnant wives.

Grumbling is not a passionate protest against society; it is an inborn talent. Grumblers are at their best in restaurants.

Within ten swift minutes a practised grumbler can take a dislike to the shape of his chair, the position of his table, the insolent way the waiter's looking at him, and the well-known fact that no foreigner can cook a simple dish without putting octopus tentacles in it.

* * *

Anne Jellicoe

A man's briefing to another on how to break down a woman's resistance –

Flattery is useful: if a woman is intelligent, make her think she's pretty; if she's pretty, make her think she's beautiful. Never let them think, never let them see you are clever and intellectual. Never be serious with a woman. Once you let a woman start thinking, the whole process takes infinitely more time. Keep her laughing, keep her talking; you can judge by her laughter, by the way she laughs, how you're getting on.

* * *

Mary Kelly

I have a horror of becoming one of those hysterical, weepy, nappy-obsessed women, who collapse when faced with an unbearable situation, rather than turn round and remove the cause. Crime is, on the whole, contrary to all that.

* * *

Joyce Kilmer (1888-1918)

> I think that I shall never see
> A poem lovely as a tree. . . .
> Poems are made by fools like me,
> But only God can make a tree.

* * *

Duchess of Kingston (1720-1788)

England is a slipshod place. The English are forever seeking amusement without finding it, whilst the French possess it without the fatigue of running after it.

* * *

Madame de Lafayette (1634-1693)

Infidelities may be forgiven, but never forgotten.

* * *

Lady Caroline Lamb (1785-1828)

On Byron –

Mad, bad and dangerous to know.

Must we adulterate truth, as they do beer?

Life, after all that has been said of its brevity, is very, very long, and more persons feel reason to complain of its slowness than of the swiftness of its course.

* * *

Mary Wilson Little

If a mosquito bite thee on one hand, give him the other – palm downward.

The penalty of success is to be bored by the attentions of people who formerly snubbed you.

The tombstone is about the only thing that can stand upright and lie on its face at the same time.

Politeness is one half good nature and the other half good lying.

There is no pleasure in having nothing to do; the fun is in having lots to do and not doing it.

In some parts of Ireland the sleep, which knows no waking, is always followed by a wake, which knows no sleeping.

It is difficult to tell which gives some couples the most happiness, the minister who marries them, or the judge who divorces them.

A youth with his first cigar makes himself sick; a youth with his first girl makes other people sick.

*   *   *

Belle Livingstone (1875-1957)

She was a foundling –

Like Moses, I wasn't born. I was found.

Of the Prince of Wales (afterwards King Edward VII), she said –

The Prince prefers a witty nobody to a titled crone.

To bait and to catch the male has always been women's first and most natural interest in life.

Men are nicer to the women they don't marry.

Figures don't lie but a liar can figure.

Perfumes and toilet water are wishy-washy, unless balanced by pipe and tweeds.

A woman gambling for a man is the finest player on earth. Not so in a game of chance. There she reveals exactly what she is holding.

Describing an actress –

She was more jewelled than a Swiss watch. A diamond dog-collar had a stranglehold on her throat.

*   *   *

Anita Loos

On Hollywood –

There isn't another spot on earth where I could obtain one tenth the mental, moral, spiritual and aesthetic joy that I get right here!

When I wake in the morning and open my newspaper, I find that the death of Eleanora Duse has been crowded into two lines at the bottom of the page by the breath-taking announcement that Tony, the Horse, has just signed a new movie contract, with a large picture of Tony, pen tied to his hoof, doing it.

In a Hollywood Studio –

THE PRODUCER: Tell the guy you got playing Disraeli to take that monocle out of his eye.

THE DIRECTOR: Do you want this picture to be historically correct or do you not?

THE PRODUCER: Not if it's bad for the box office. A monocle may be historically correct, but it makes the guy look like a gigolo. And the public would think the Queen's got him hanging around for no good reason.

The Star to the Publicity Man –

Nobody before realised that I loved mountains, and birds, and bees, and flowers! Why, I never even knew it myself *until you told me*!

Confession of a Movie Star –

I started to read a book called *The Story of Madame Curie*, the eminent Pole, who led such an extraordinary love life with her own husband, and also got herself played by Greer Garson and discovered Radium. . . . I didn't bother to read all those pages about Radium, because things that are written outside Hollywood always place the emphasis on the wrong thing. For instance, in Hollywood we realise that those scientists keep right on discovering better and better things all the time.

A leader of public thought in Hollywood wouldn't have sufficient mental acumen anywhere else to hold down a place in the bread line!

*   *   *

Clare Boothe Luce

Nature abhors a virgin – a frozen asset.

If a woman's got any instincts, she feels when her husband's off the reservation.

Practically nobody ever misses a clever woman.

Motherly advice: don't confide in your girl friend.

I don't feel sorry for any woman who thinks the world owes her breakfast in bed.

Be intelligent, fair maid, and let who will be good.

A woman's best protection is a little money of her own.

There's nothing that keeps a woman so in the dumps as sleeping in a bed with old associations.

It's matrimonial suicide to be jealous when you have a really good reason.

Pride – that's a luxury a woman in love can't afford.

Speaking of a friend expecting her fifth child –

That marriage is what you may call an *enceinte cordiale*.

* * *

Duchesse de Luynes

When a Count, a religious fanatic, announced that the Virgin Mary visited him nightly, the Duchess whispered to a friend –

He is luckier than Joseph was.

* * *

Anne O'Hare McCormick (1882-1954)

When she was interviewing Hitler, he foamed at the mouth and screamed –

'What are you doing about the Jews in America?' She replied, 'We think we're just as good as they are.'

*   *   *

'Madame' (1652-1722)

Title given to Elizabeth-Charlotte, Princess Palatine and Duchess of Orleans, wife of Philippe, only brother of Louis XIV of France.

Celibacy is the better stake, since the best husband is not worth a fig.

The King [Louis XIV] thinks that he is a saint, because he no longer beds with any young woman.

A young woman who allows herself to be kissed and caressed goes the rest of the way too.

On long Church services –

We listen to a long High Mass for two hours. If all that doesn't please God better than it pleases me, I think the priests are much to be pitied.

Forbidden fruits taste better than those that are allowed.

Very few French people care a scrap about ancestry, but money is respected by everyone.

Cardinal de Bouillon is dead. He was worthless; that is the best funeral oration that can be given.

On French women –

The lowest servant girl thinks that she is quite capable of directing the State.

*　*　*

Katherine Mansfield (1888-1923)

Regret is an appalling waste of energy; you can't build on it; it's good only for wallowing in.

I have nothing to say to 'charming' women. I feel like a cat among tigers.

*　*　*

Elizabeth Marbury (1856-1933)

A caress is better than a career.

The richer your friends, the more they will cost you.

No influence so quickly converts a radical into a reactionary as does his election to power.

Years in themselves mean nothing. How we live means everything.

* * *

Duchess of Marlborough (1660-1744)

Prithee don't talk to me about books. The only books I know are men and cards.

* * *

Daphne du Maurier

Her rule of Life –

Writers should be read, but neither seen nor heard.

Every book is like a purge. When one comes to the end of it, one pulls the plug, and finish.

* * *

Elsa Maxwell (1883-1963)

Called by Bernard Shaw 'The eighth wonder of the world'.
Definition of being coy –

A pose as ridiculous as a grass skirt on Venus de Milo.

Enemies to me are the *sauce piquant* to my dish of life!

There was a running gag that I always travelled with fourteen trunks and a hat box – the trunks for the press cuttings, and the hat box for another dress. A base *canard*. I didn't own another dress . . . my vanity was as negative as my bank account.

The cocktail party is easily the worst invention since castor oil.

More than one woman since Lot's wife has betrayed herself by looking back.

No one ever went broke in Hollywood underestimating the intelligence of the public.

On Hollywood –

The compulsion that drove people to the bar was obvious. It was to escape from the cultural vacuum in which they existed. An arrival from outer space who attempted to discuss politics, the arts, personalities in the news, would soon be talking to himself.

On being a celebrity –

One thing you don't need is looks. I have been compared in and out of print to creation's most loathsome forms of life. I've always been laughed at but I've never been ignored.

Celebrities are human, after all. Occasionally they sit around together just being people – but, I admit, not for long.

Keep your talent in the dark and you'll never be insulted.

Lunching with Dorothy Parker and a man, who hated Elsa Maxwell. The man, in reply to a question, said –

'I'm going to stay with an artist, Augustus John; you wouldn't know him.'
'Elsa knows him well,' said Dorothy Parker, 'she calls him Augustus Jack.'

I never liked the idea of sex. I married the world. The world is my husband. Sex is the most tiring thing in the world.

Position is only what you are yourself, and what you give to those around you.

* * *

Caren Meyer

Whoever perpetrated the mathematical inaccuracy 'Two can live as cheaply as one' has a lot to answer for.

* * *

Edna St Vincent Millay (1892-1950)

FIRST FIG

My candle burns at both ends;
   It will not last the night;
But ah, my foes, and oh, my friends . . .
   It gives a lovely light!

* * *

Nancy Mitford

In England, if you are a Duchess, you don't need to be well-dressed — it would be thought quite eccentric.

English women are elegant until they are ten years old, and perfect on grand occasions.

An aristocracy in a republic is like a chicken whose head has been cut off; it may run about in a lovely way, but in fact it is dead.

The English lord knows himself to be such a very genuine article that, when looking for a wife, he can rise above such baubles as *seize quartiers*. Kind hearts, in his view, are more than coronets, and large tracts of town property more than Norman blood. He marries for love, and is rather inclined to love where money is.

Americans relate all effort, all work and all life itself to the dollar. The English seldom sit happily chatting for hours on end about pounds.

* * *

Elisabeth Montagu (1720-1800)

If things were as in Aesop's days, when beasts could talk, the country might be a place of conversation.

To the Dean of Canterbury –

I have lately studied my own foibles, and have found that I should make a very silly wife, and an extremely foolish mother, and so have resolved, as far as is consistent with deference to reason and advice, never to trouble any man, or to spoil any children.

(She married Edward Montagu, MP, in 1742.)

Solomon said of laughter, 'What is it?' and of mirth, 'What does it?' Vanity and a good set of teeth would have taught him the ends and purposes of laughing.

Reason for the success of her parties –

No idiots were ever invited.

* * *

Lady Mary Wortley Montagu (1689-1762)

Had a great reputation for scholarship. Held salons in London, Rome, Venice, and Constantinople.

It goes far towards reconciling me being a woman when I reflect that I am thus in no danger of marrying one.

I give myself sometimes admirable advice, but I am incapable of taking it.

Remember my unalterable maxim – when we love, we have always something to say.

It is extremely silly to submit to ill fortune.

To my extreme mortification, I grow wiser every day.

Of George I –

In private life he would be called an honest blockhead.

Of Prince George (later George II) –

He looked on all men and women as creatures he might kiss or kick for his diversion.

Life is too short for any distant aim; and cold the dull reward of any future.

* * *

Hannah More (1745-1833)

> He liked those literary cooks
> Who skim the cream of others' books;
> And ruin half an author's graces
> By plucking *bons mots* from their places.

For you'll never mend your fortunes, nor help the just
cause,
By breaking of windows, or breaking of laws.

* * *

Ethel Watts Mumford (1878-1940)

Don't take the will for the deed; get the deed.

God gives us our relatives; thank God we can choose our friends.

Think of your ancestors and your posterity, and you will never marry.

In the midst of life we are in debt.

It is better to make friends fast than to make fast friends.

When folly is bliss, 'tis ignorance to be otherwise.

Knowledge is power if you know it about the right person.

A man of courage never needs weapons, but he may need bail.

Oh wad some power the giftie gie us to see some people before they see us.

You may lead an ass to knowledge but you cannot make him think.

One good turn deserves applause.

The greatest possession is self-possession.

Pleasant company is always accepted.

Advice to parents –

Cast not your girls before swains.

Women change their minds a dozen times a day – that's why they are so clean-minded.

Kind hearts are more than coronets – few girls can afford to have either.

Shut your mouth and open your eyes – and you'll need nothing to make you wise.

* * *

Margot Naylor

If every successful man needs a woman behind him, every successful woman needs at least three men.

* * *

Madame Necker (1739-1794)

It is often a sign of wit not to show it, and not to see that others want it.

Women's failings were given them by Nature so as to try men's virtues.

Men should rise above prejudices, but women should submit to them.

* * *

Florence Nightingale, OM (1820-1910)

Commenting on the hospital at Scutari (1855) –

The vermin might, if they had but unity of purpose, carry off the four miles of beds on their backs, and march with them into the War Office, Horse Guards, SW.

I love this world and I don't want any other.

* * *

Edna O'Brien

When anyone asks me about the Irish character, I say – look at the trees. Maimed, stark and misshapen, but ferociously tenacious. The Irish have got gab but are too touchy to be humorous. Me too.

A woman's need to be circumferenced by a man is as strong and biologic as ever.

For a sensitive and aware person, sleeping around is the most wearying and diminishing of pastimes. Only a bullock or a mechanic could persist in it.

I have some women friends but I prefer men. Don't trust women. There is a built-in competition between women.

* * *

Ouida (Maria de la Ramée) (1839-1908)

With peaches and women, it's only the side next to the sun that's tempting; if you find acid in either, leave them for the downy blush of another!

* * *

Dorothy Parker (1893-1967)

General Review of the Sex Situation –

> Woman wants monogamy,
> Man delights in novelty.
> Love is woman's moon and sun;
> Man has other forms of fun.
> Woman lives but in her lord;
> Count to ten, and man is bored.
> With this gist and sum of it,
> What earthly good can come of it?

On an actress's performance –

She ran the whole gamut of the emotions from A to B.

Men seldom make passes at girls who wear glasses.

*   *   *

Catherine Parr (1512-1548)

On Henry's proposal of marriage –

O Sire, it were better to be your mistress than your wife.

Intent on saving her neck –

Your Majesty, I have always held it preposterous for a woman to instruct her lord, and if I have ever presumed to differ with your Highness, it was to obtain information for my own comfort, and in the hope of profiting by your Majesty's learning.

* * *

Madame Roland (1754-1793)

O liberty! O liberty! What crimes are committed in thy name.

* * *

Helen Rowland (1875-1950)

Woman: the peg on which the wit hangs his jest, the preacher his text, the cynic his grouch, and the sinner his justification.

* * *

George Sand (1804-1876)

We cannot tear out a simple page of our life, but we can throw the whole book on the fire.

Simplicity is the most difficult thing to secure in this world; it is the last limit of experience and the last effort of genius.

Art for the sake of art itself is an idle sentence. Art for the sake of truth, for the sake of what is beautiful and good – that is the creed I seek.

On Women –

Flattery is the yoke with which to make their light and ardent heads submissive.

*   *   *

Sappho (c 600 BC)

Love is a cunning weaver of fantasies and fables.

When a wrathful emotion comes to the breast, beware of speech that is idle.

> Be kind, be loving, and anon,
> You will be lovely too.

> Wealth without virtue is a dangerous quest;
> Who holds them mingled is supremely blest.

Justice is the fairest thing, health is the best, but the sweetest of all is to find your lover.

*   *   *

Anne Scott-James

The very rich have an obligation to the rest of the world to amuse us. In an age when too many of the rich are over-modest, running round in mini-cars and wearing fake jewellery, I applaud the Richard Burtons for spending their money in the grand manner.

To hire a two hundred-ton yacht for two months as a kennel for your doggies shows true star quality.

I am a staunch believer in having one's cake and eating it, a principle I have followed greedily throughout my life.

* * *

Madeleine de Scudéry (1607-1701)

He who reveals his secret to an indiscreet friend, is more indiscreet than the indiscreet one.

Repentance is hardly ever voluntary, and we might say that it is the invariable sequel to the failure of our enterprise.

Reason is a weak antagonist against love.

* * *

Madame de Sévigné (1626-1696)

It's the fine rain that soaks us through.

A devoted friendship is never without anxiety.

The best things are disgusting, when they are thrown at our heads.

* * *

Cornelia Otis Skinner

I am no feminist. I don't want to do man's work. . . . Why is it a foregone conclusion that timetables are something for men only, and that it is unmanly or ungallant to stand by and allow a woman to look up a train?

Nothing can depress me more rapidly nor more hopelessly than a book on how to be happy. . . . If uplift books cast me down, those of pessimism and despair work the other way. I have just finished Dostoevsky's *The Idiot*, and I haven't felt so bucked in weeks.

* * *

Muriel Spark

Do you think it pleases a man when he looks into a woman's eyes and sees a reflection of the British Museum Reading Room?

One should only see a psychiatrist out of boredom.

* * *

Edith Stein

One cannot expect a little hare to behave like a lion.

* * *

Gertrude Stein (1874-1946)

I have the failing of my tribe. I believe in the sacred rites of conversation even when it is a monologue.

If a thing can be done, why do it?

Any copy is a bad copy.

War is never fatal but always lost.

Everybody gets so much information all day long that they lose their common sense.

*   *   *

Han Suyin

Truth, like surgery, may hurt, but it cures.

One should never condemn what one cannot understand.

Heaven equalises all things.

You only understand the present when it is past.

There is not anything stronger in the world than tenderness.

It's only big enough people who can afford, occasionally, to be untrammelled by ordinary prejudice.

On Journalists –

The great dispensers of up-to-the-minute unrest to the millions. *Folie de grandeur* is their occupational disease.

* * *

Carmen Sylva (1843-1916)

An aphorism is like a bee, fully burdened with gold, but with a sting attached.

* * *

Empress Maria Teresa (1717-1780)

To her son, King Joseph II –

Beware of enjoying mean acts.

* * *

Angela Thirkell (1890-1961)

The great thing in life is not to be able to do things, because then they are done for you.

Never economise on luxuries.

If one cannot invent a really convincing lie, it is often better to stick to the truth.

* * *

Melesina Trench (1768-1827)

On London Society –

Like flies caught in a bottle of honey, all are smothered in disgusting sweets, and all are trying to rise above each other, no matter how.

*   *   *

Carolyn Wells (1869-1942)

A fool and his money are soon married.

A little debutante is a dangerous thing.

Proposals make cowards of us all.

There's no fool like a bold fool.

The longest way round is the sweetest way home.

Kisses speak louder than words.

People who live in glass houses shouldn't hold hands.

Where there's a will there's a wedding.

Epigrams cover a multitude of sins.

The wages of sin is alimony.

Of two evils choose the prettier.

It's a wise child that owes its own father.

A guilty conscience is the mother of invention.

Actions lie louder than words.

Circumstances alter faces.

He who loves and runs away, may live to love another day.

Man's importunity is woman's opportunity.

We should live and learn; but by the time we've learned, it's too late to live.

*   *   *

Katharine Whitehorn

The people who get on are the people who can get their mind off their own predicament and think of someone else.

The one social lapse for which there is no forgiveness is forgetting people's names – it makes them feel that they are small and unmemorable.

The great rule is not to talk about money with people who have much more or much less than you.

Definition of a lesbian film star: One who wouldn't sleep with the photographer.

Whereas a lot of men used to ask for conversation when they really wanted sex, nowadays they often feel obliged to ask for sex even when they really want conversation.

Nice people don't swank, they don't make the rest of us feel small; they don't pass on our secrets or say bloody in public or tell you how much money they make or talk with their mouth full.

If you scorn anyone below what you think is your own social rating, you'll be in trouble if it ever goes down.

Men will try to use secretaries as status symbols. They hire them for ornamental reasons. Every time a young one leaves to get married, they swear they'll go for someone older and steadier. Then they go right ahead and hire the next pretty face with 40-40 speeds.

* * *

Elsie de Wolfe (Lady Mendl) (?1858-1950)

About the date of her birth –

In my philosophy, taking toll of the years is a destructive process.

Only those are unwise who have never dared to be fools.

Her mother's advice –

Be pretty if you can; be witty if you must; but be amiable always.

* * *

Virginia Woolf (1882-1941)

The merest schoolgirl, when she falls in love, has Shakespeare or Keats to speak her mind for her; but let a sufferer try to describe a pain in his head to a doctor and language at once runs dry.

* * *

Elizabeth Wordsworth (1840-1932)

> If all the good people were clever,
> And all clever people were good,
> The world would be nicer than ever
> We thought that it possibly could.
> But somehow, 'tis seldom or never
> The two hit it off as they should;
> The good are so harsh to the clever,
> The clever so rude to the good!

The Dames

Ivy Compton-Burnett, DBE

I like fact to be fact and fiction to be fiction; it disturbs me not to know where one ends and the other begins.

The primary function of a novel is to tell a story, and a story that makes sense to reasonable people.

On being compared with Jane Austen –

Cannot two cooks make the same light pastry without one necessarily being under the influence of the other?

Speaking of plots for novels –

I find real life no help at all. Real life seems to have no plots.

People who jest always, jest not at all.

* * *

Gladys Cooper, DBE

Family is the best part of my life; and the other part is my work. I've never made a comeback. I've never been away.

* * *

Adeline Genée-Isitt, DBE

To help people pronounce her name –

The name is pronounced as in 'I sit, you stand', not as in 'Is it?' I am a fact, not a query.

* * *

Barbara Hepworth, DBE

Life will always insist on begetting life.

Of Architects –

We have forgotten that it is more important to put up something which does justice to our time, than to prepare ourselves for mass extermination. . . . What we really suffer from is spiritual malnutrition.

* * *

Madge Kendall, DBE (1849-1945)

Asked, when elderly, how she managed to look so well –

I try to fill up my wrinkles with intelligence.

Comment on Birth Control –

> Sister Susie built her hopes
> On the books of Marie Stopes.
> But I fear from her condition,
> She must have read the wrong edition.

* * *

Laura Knight, DBE, RA

Commenting on her circus pictures –

I was not, as most people think, born in a circus, suckled by an elephant, and, as a baby, tossed on the feet of an acrobat.

When I travelled with the circus, I always shared cheap lodgings with two performers, man and wife.
My title 'Dame' was little known in those days and the landladies always thought I was a pantomime Dame.

* * *

Alicia Markova, DBE

Describes her life as –

A series of pirouettes from one city to another.

Men are a little afraid of a woman who is only alive with her own personal instinct.

On being a wallflower at dances –

Men are embarrassed to dance with a ballerina.

*   *   *

Nellie Melba, GBE (1861-1931)

The first rule in opera is the first rule in life: see to everything yourself. You must not only sing, you must not only act, you must be stage manager, press agent, artistic adviser, mother, father, sister, all rolled into one. . . . It would be a good thing if you have a bed fixed up in one of the boxes, so that you will be always on the spot.

Pleading for International music –

Music is not written in red, white and blue. It is written in the heart's blood of the composer.

It is a strange irony that I may go down to posterity as a peach or a piece of toast.

* * *

Marie Rambert, DBE

On being made a Dame –

It's the dame-ing of the Shrew.

* * *

Flora Robson, DBE

Of course you use sex in your work. People without any aren't very good at work either.

In modern plays women are there to be shouted at.

* * *

Edith Sitwell, DBE (1887-1964)

I am resigned to the fact that people who don't know me loathe me. It is because I am a woman who dares to write poetry.

Speaking of her strange manner of dressing –

If I walked around in modern clothes, I would make people doubt the existence of God.

To an American who asked 'Why do you call yourself Dame?' she snapped –

I don't – the Queen does.

I am one of those unhappy persons who inspire bores to the highest flights of their art.

To offensive American journalists –

I cannot call you geese, because geese saved the Capitol, and your cackling would awaken nobody. I cannot call you asses, because Balaam's constant companion saw and recognised an angel.

* * *

Marie Tempest, DBE (1864-1942)

I never allow myself to be bored, because boredom is ageing. If you live in the past you grow old, and dull, and dusty. It's very nice, of course, to be young and beautiful; but there are other qualities, thank God.

* * *

Ellen Terry, GBE (1848-1928)

Speaking on modern actresses –

A young girl goes into a play, becomes a success. She is boosted to the skies.

We even learn what toothpaste she uses. Then in about another week, somebody else turns up. The first girl is forgotten. Even the toothpaste is forgotten.

* * *

Maggie Teyte, DBE

Touring in America with the Boston Opera Company, I was given a dressing-room with a star painted on the door, which was the custom in those days.

When I opened the door and went inside, I found the following rhyme written in lipstick on the large mirror:
>'Twinkle, twinkle, little star,
>>Who the hell do you think you are?'

What a pity that more mirrors are not scribbled on these days!

* * *

Sybil Thorndike, DBE

On theatre critics –

You must allow critics to say what they like, but the poor darlings have so many plays to see night after night that they get bored.

One shouldn't be sorry one has attempted to say something new – never, never.

* * *

Irene Vanbrugh, DBE (1872-1949)

Any young man who meets a woman with charm is aware of something unusual. He may like it or dislike it, but he knows at once that it is different from what he is accustomed to in women today.

I can't help thinking of that old saying – you don't lose your taste for the real salmon, although you can afford only the canned variety.

*   *   *

Rebecca West, DBE

He is every other inch a gentleman.

It is a thankless task to be the perfect embodiment of a transition period.

One could imagine her giving Pavlova a few hints on dancing, because she had such a success as a skirt-dancer at bazaars in her youth.

Anonymous

Under this heading, we have collected the witticisms that have been attributed to many notable women, but, being honest, they have disclaimed the credit for having said or written them.

Brevity is the soul of lingerie.

The only 'ism' Hollywood believes in is plagiarism.

Women don't become bluestockings until men are no longer interested in the colour of their stockings.

Love makes time pass – and time makes love pass.

The greatest liar is he who talks most of himself.

No man is clever enough to lick himself on the back.

Men run the world. Why argue or quarrel with them when a sniffle will do the trick?

Hollywood is the place where inferior people make superior people feel inferior.

A rat is a beauty in the eyes of its mother.

Before marriage a girl has to kiss her man to hold him; after marriage, she has to hold him to kiss him.

Before marriage, she knows all the answers; after marriage, she knows all the questions.

Before marriage a man yearns for a woman; after marriage, the 'Y' is silent.

A lady is apt to think a man speaks so much reason while he is commending her, that she has much ado to believe him in the wrong when he is making love to her.

From a 'Lady of Fashion', 1780 –

Women in London are like rich silks; they are out of fashion a great while before they wear out.

Never speak what you don't think, or all you do.

Love and Marriage

Love, which is only an episode in the life of man, is the entire history of woman's life.
Madame de Staël (1766–1817)

Margot Asquith (1864-1945)

When a man threatens to commit suicide after you have refused him, you may be quite sure that he is a vain, petty fellow, or a great goose.

To marry a man out of pity is folly. It is the height of vanity to suppose that you can make an honest man of anyone.

* * *

Mary Astell (1668-1731)

Women marry off in haste, for perhaps if they took time to consider and reflect upon it, they seldom would marry.

* * *

LOVE AND MARRIAGE

Jane Austen (1775-1817)

All the privilege I claim for my own sex . . . is that of loving longest, when existence or when hope is gone.

* * *

Aphra Behn (1640-1689)

Oh, what a dear, ravishing thing is the beginning of an Amour!

Love ceases to be a pleasure when it ceases to be a secret.

* * *

Mrs Oliver Belmont

Her daughter, Consuelo, married the Duke of Marlborough.

Every woman should marry twice. The first time for money, the second time for love.

* * *

Drusilla Beyfus

Marriage, I am convinced, is going to be the last subject to be effectively computerised.

* * *

Countess of Blessington

Love matches are formed by people who pay for a month of honey with a life of vinegar.

Love and enthusiasm are always ridiculous, when not reciprocated by their objects.

Love in France is a comedy; in England a tragedy; in Italy an *opera seria*; and in Germany a melodrama.

* * *

M E Braddon (1837-1915)

Why is it so difficult to love wisely, so easy to love too well?

* * *

Queen Caroline (1683-1737)

On her deathbed, she urged her husband, King George II, to marry again. . . . He replied that he would have mistresses. To which she answered –

That shouldn't hamper your marrying.

* * *

Barbara Cartland

Getting married in our civilisation is rather like getting born. It is a matter of luck. Staying married is a work of art.

The passion and starry-eyed joys of the honeymoon are but callow experiments in a search for the magnificent which lies beyond the horizon.

In marriage, as in every other activity of living, we must seek new ideas, new angles, fresh inspiration. The coffin of any marriage is boredom.

* * *

Catherine of Genoa (1477-1510)

Love makes the crooked seem straight.

* * *

Ilka Chase

Love affairs without marriage are not devoid of pleasure – they can be wonderfully fresh and zestful, rather like crisp green lettuce with a sharp dressing. But they need every advantage they can claim to compensate for the inconvenience, insecurity and deception usually implicit in their practice, and for the heartache involved in their dissolution.

* * *

THE WIT OF WOMEN

Christina of Sweden (1626-1689)

Life is too short to be able to love as one should.

Marriage is the sovereign remedy against love.

We can have only one real love, but many tender friendships.

Love engenders jealousy, but jealousy kills love.

*   *   *

Marie Corelli (1855-1924)

There is no wealth but love.

Men are so silly. They don't – or won't – realise that it is not money, or clothes, or jewels their wives want, but tenderness, courtesy, understanding, and affection.

Many marriages fail because couples cease to be sweethearts.

*   *   *

Clemence Dane

A monogamous marriage is a finer way of living at its best than any other type of marriage.

A bad marriage is like an infectious disease in a house: for the sake of the whole community such a disease must be stamped out.

* * *

Eleonora Duse (1859-1924)

Silence is one of the many noble sides of love.

* * *

Queen Elizabeth I (1533-1603)

In answer to a request by the Speaker and the Lower House that she should marry –

It will be quite sufficient for the memorial of my name and for my glory if, when I die, an inscription be engraved on a marble tomb, saying, 'Here lieth Elizabeth, which reigned a virgin, and died a virgin.'

I would rather be a beggar and single, than a Queen and married. . . . I should call the wedding-ring the yoke-ring.

When a woman remains single, the world assumes that there must be something wrong about her, that she has some discreditable reason for it.

* * *

Ninon de l'Enclos (1620-1705)

Parisienne of good family, she shocked her contemporaries by her mockery of sacred subjects.

Admired by Cardinal Richelieu, she visited him, dressed as a page. Her favourite maxims –

Feminine virtue is nothing but a convenient masculine invention.

Love is no more than a play of whim and vanity.

Much more genius is needed to make love than to command armies.

Love never dies of starvation, but often of indigestion.

The resistance of a woman is not always proof of her virtue, but more often of her experience.

A love affair is, of all dramas, that in which the acts are longest, the interval shortest – and how can these be filled by cultivating one's talent?

Men lose more conquests by their own awkwardness than by any virtue in the woman.

Wit is very dangerous in friendship. It is not enough to be wise – one must please as well.

Gossip, like ennui, is born of idleness.

That which is striking and beautiful is not always good, but that which is good is always beautiful.

When women pass thirty, they first forget their age; when forty, they forget that they ever remembered it.

A sensible woman should never fall in love without her heart's consent, nor marry without that of her reason.

Without grace, beauty is an unbaited hook.

Platonic love is an illusion; it does not exist in nature.

If a man gives a woman wealth, it is only a proof of his generosity; but if he gives her his time, it is proof of his love.

In love-making, feigning lovers succeed much better than the really devoted.

* * *

Madame Fée

However dull a woman may be, she will understand all there is of love; however intelligent a man may be, he will never know but half of it.

* * *

Yvette Guilbert

Don't get married stupidly, just to avoid celibacy! That is shame of body and bitterness of soul.

The love of woman is supernatural. Man feels nothing like it. A woman will cling to a man who crucifies her – worse yet to a man who bores her.

Woman can never be independent. No matter what a man may be – drunkard, gambler, thief; whether he be indelicate, a liar, a hypocrite, or cruel, or evil, or sick, unclean, malodorous – there will always be found one woman, nay ten women, who will lavish upon him their smiles, their kisses, all their gifts.

* * *

Texas Guinan

Contemplating her fourth marriage –

I've been married once on the level, and twice in America.

* * *

Lady Caroline Lamb (1785-1828)

Love, like other arts, requires experience.

* * *

'Madame' (1652-1722)

Love is a sauce which makes all dishes palatable.

* * *

Princess Mathilde (1820-1904)

On her cousin, Louis Napoleon –

If I'd ever married him, I'd have had to crack his head open to find out if there was anything in it.

Marry your lover, it's the only way to regain your liberty.

*   *   *

Daphne du Maurier

On romance –

I don't know what the word means. It sounds as if it's something to do with knights in shining armour.

*   *   *

Elsa Maxwell (1883-1963)

Seeing unhappiness in the marriage of friends, I was content to have chosen music and laughter as a substitute for a husband.

*   *   *

Nancy Mitford

To fall in love you have to be in the state of mind for it to take, like a disease.

People fall in love with the most extraordinary people. But that's one of the things that makes life so interesting and amusing.

I think Freud has spoilt everything. He's taken away so much of the glamour... In the 18th century, love existed, but so did other things, such as hunting, feasting and the pleasures of the mind. Love wasn't the be-all and end-all because people hadn't read Freud and didn't know it had to be.

* * *

Edna O'Brien

Marriage is a mutual blackmail. If it has to be undone, it just leads to a great legal event. . . . Why shouldn't one realise it is a temporary state? Life is temporary.

* * *

Madame de Pinzieux

Curiosity has destroyed more women than love.

* * *

Helen Rowland (1875-1950)

Before marriage, a man will lie awake thinking about something you said; after marriage, he'll fall asleep before you finish saying it.

Half a love is better than none.

LOVE AND MARRIAGE

When you see what some girls marry, you realise how they must hate to work for a living.

Love, the quest; marriage, the conquest; divorce, the inquest.

Marriage: a souvenir of love.

* * *

Madame de Sartory

More than half your friend is lost to you, when he falls in love.

* * *

Madame de Staël (1766-1817)

Love is an emblem of eternity; it confounds all notion of time, effaces all memory of a beginning, all fear of an end.

One may love a second time, but the happiness of confiding one's whole soul, one can never find again.

* * *

Marie Stopes (1880-1958)

The best answer I ever saw to that cynical question 'Why marry?' is because love commands!

* * *

Han Suyin

Love is a many-splendoured thing.

It is the illusion of all lovers to think themselves unique and their words immortal.

* * *

Gillian Tindall

Not many people of either sex are complete Jekylls and Hydes. You normally have opportunity to notice that someone is a self-centred louse (or an hysterical bitch) before the marital knot is tied, and if you feel you *haven't* had enough opportunity, then don't marry yet!

* * *

Madame de la Tour

In love, as in all other matters, experience is a doctor who comes too late.

* * *

Marguerite de Valois (1553-1615)

In love, as in war, a fortress that parleys is half taken.

Mistresses and Courtesans

'Courtesans used to know more about the soul of men than any philosopher. The art is lost in the fog of snobbism and false respectability.'

Elsa Schiaparelli

Madame du Barry (1741-1793)

Illegitimate daughter of a cook, she became a favourite mistress of Louis XV, who declared that 'she is the only woman in France who makes me forget I am a sexagenarian'.

Bewildered by a début as a young girl in a refined brothel, she complained of the affected manners to her mother, who replied –

Don't worry, men tire of always eating capons and delicate fruit; a good cabbage now and then delights them.

Small kindnesses are the food of friendship.

*   *   *

Catherine the Great (1729-1796)

Writing of the legitimacy of her son and heir –

I was attractive. That was the halfway house to temptation, and in such cases human nature does the rest. To tempt and to be tempted is much the same thing.

To Prince Potemkin –

The trouble is that my heart is loath to remain even one hour without love. . . . Let the mind rest in order that the feelings should be free.

*   *   *

Marquise du Defand (1697-1780)

Had a famous salon, and many lovers. In her seventieth year, blind, she met Horace Walpole, and a strange love affair developed with a man she had never seen. When Walpole criticised her romantic transport, she replied –

It is better to be a bad original, than a good copy.

Only affection, absurdity, and pretension shock me.

Women are never stronger than when they arm themselves with their weakness.

*   *   *

Juliette Drouet (1806-1883)

Inspiration of many of the poems of her lover, Victor Hugo –

I love you – that means everything.

Suspicion leads to contempt, and when that exists, no real love is possible.

To Hugo's comment on her short letters, she replied –

Fine unguents are contained in small boxes; great love in trivial words.

Love is a splendid stereoscope. It can even convert black jealousy into white confidence. My faith in the power of love amounts to superstition.

He whose heart is younger than his years suffers all the sorrows of his age.

*   *   *

Countess d'Esparbes (Mistress of Louis XV)

During their first night, Louis said reproachfully –

'You have slept with every one of my subjects!'
She answered bashfully, 'Oh, Sire!'
'You have had the Duc de Choiseul.'
'He is so powerful.'
'The Maréchal de Richelieu.'
'He is so witty.'
'Monville.'
'He has such beautiful legs.'

'Very well. But what about the Duc d'Aumont, who has nothing of all this?'

'Ah, Sire, he – he is so devoted to Your Majesty!'

* * *

Mrs Fitzherbert (1756-1837)

The mistress of the Prince of Wales, afterwards George IV. It is generally believed that a marriage took place between them. She always held it was valid.

Advice is like a jest which every fool is offering another, and yet won't take himself.

No law is made for love.

Love is not in our choice, but in our fate.

* * *

Nell Gwynne (1650-1687)

'Come hither, you little bastard!' she cried to her son Charles in the hearing of his father, the King. When Charles rebuked her, she replied, 'I have no better name to call him by.' Soon after, the boy was created Baron of Headington and Earl of Burford.

When Charles II had become unpopular because of his Catholic mistress, and people hurled stones at the Royal coach, Nell put her head out and said, 'Pray good people, be silent. I'm the Protestant whore.'

* * *

Henrietta Howard (Countess of Suffolk) (1681-1767)

For many years mistress of George II.

I think every man is in the wrong who talks to a woman of dying for her; for the only women who can have received a benefit from such a protestation are the widows.

I cannot much wonder that men are always so liberal in making presents of their hearts. Let us consider the ingredients that make up the heart of a man. It is composed of dissimulation, self-love, vanity, inconstancy, equivocation, and such fine qualities. A man's heart never wants the outward appearance of truth and sincerity. Every lover's heart is so finely varnished with them, that it is almost impossible to distinguish the true from the false ones. The false ones have generally the finest gloss. Therefore, let everyone who expects an equivalent for his heart be provided with a false one, which will burn, flame, bleed, pant, sigh, and receive as many darts, and appear altogether as charming as the true one.

Successful love is very unlike Heaven, because you may have success one hour and lose it the next. Heaven is unchangeable; who can say so of love, of lovers?

In love, there are as many Heavens as there are women;

so that if a man be so unhappy as to lose one Heaven, he need not throw himself headlong into Hell.

If a woman be neither like angel nor devil, what is she like? The only thing that is like a woman is – another woman.

To Lord Peterborough –

A man cannot give a heart for a heart that has none to give. Consider, my Lord, you have but one heart, and then consider whether you have a right to dispose of it. Is there not a lady in Paris, who is convinced that nobody has it but herself? Did you not bequeath it to another lady in Turin? At Venice, you disposed of it to six or seven; and again you parted with it at Naples and Sicily. I am therefore obliged, my lord, to believe that one who disposes of his heart in so profuse a manner is like a juggler, who seems to fling away a piece of money, but still has it in his own keeping.

*   *   *

Julie de Lespinasse (1732-1762)

Illegitimate daughter of the Comtesse d'Albou, she established herself as the darling of the Parisian intellectuals. Her last and most ardent love affair was with the Court favourite, Comte de Guibert.

Her popular maxims –

I love to live and I live to love.

The logic of the heart is absurd.

There is little pleasure and no glory in living for a single object. When one reigns only in one heart, one does not reign in public opinion.

A woman would be in despair, if Nature had formed her as fashion makes her appear.

Everything in the world is valued and paid for in terms of money – except love.

There is a self-evident axiom, that she who is born a beauty is half married.

*   *   *

Belle Livingstone (1875-1957)

A courtesan and a mistress are types as far apart as the poles. Anyone can become a mistress; one has to be born a courtesan.

*   *   *

Comtesse de Loynes (d 1908)

Mistress of Prince Napoleon (son of King Jerome), of Dumas fils and of Flaubert.

She once asked Clemenceau –

Is it necessary to have read Spinoza in order to make out a laundry list?

Speaking of a much younger lover (Jules Lemaître, one of France's immortals) –

I am rewarming myself with his youth.

* * *

Marquise de Maintenon (1635-1719)

I have been too far from and too near to greatness to know what it is.

When two mistresses of Louis XIV – the Marquise de Maintenon and the Marquise de Montespan – passed one another on the Queen's staircase at Versailles, Madame de Maintenon said –

You are going down, Madame, I am going up.

Secret of her influence over Louis XIV –

I always send him away despondent but never in despair.

* * *

Caroline (La Belle) Otero (1868-1965)

My self-respect and my jealous nature will not permit me to share any man with another woman.

Even since my childhood I have been accustomed to see the face of every man who passed me light up with desire. Many women will be disgusted to hear that I have always taken this as homage. Is it despicable to be the flower whose perfume people long to inhale, the fruit they long to taste?

On receiving a priceless jewel from a hideous lover –

On such basis one can't call a man ugly.

Her advice to the youthful Colette (the famous writer) –

'Remember, little one, that there's a moment in the life of every man when he opens wide his palm.'
'The moment of passion?' asked Colette.
'No,' laughed Otero, 'the moment when you twist his wrist.'

* * *

Madame Récamier (1777-1849)

Mistress of Chateaubriand, who described her as 'half lover, half virgin'.

Of a lover –

Neither he nor I were passionate enough to need to be alone with each other.

I adore tolerance, and I would cease to adore God, if I had belief in Hell.

* * *

Madame de Rieux (d 1587)

Mistress of King Henry III of France.

Flatter woman's conceit if you would win her; she will always value that.

* * *

George Sand (1804-1876)

She made popular the theory that love as an end justifies any means. Among her lovers were the poet Alfred de Musset and Chopin. No lover ever left her. It was she who tired first of the affair.

Nobody on earth loves more than I, because I love without being ashamed of the reason why I love.

Our life is composed of love, and not to love is not to live.

Love is a bad thing, or at least a dangerous trial. Glory is empty, and matrimony hateful.

Love, fidelity, maternity, are the most necessary, the

most important, and the most sacred things in the life of a woman.

The ugly wretch who buys his pleasure does not make love. It is against nature, for it is not desire that brings young girls into the arms of the old and ugly.

Whoever has loved knows all that life contains of sorrow and joy.

* * *

Madame de Staël (1766-1817)

Mistress of Benjamin Constant.

Wit consists in knowing the resemblance of things which differ, and the difference of things which are alike.

Seated between the beautiful Madame Récamier and the plain Madame de Staël, the astronomer Lalande said, 'How happy I am to find myself between wit and beauty'.
'And without possessing either,' came Madame de Staël's prompt reply.

Genius is sexless.

A man in love is like a sparrow caught with birdlime; the more he struggles, the more he is entangled.

Mental recreation is the remedy for heartache.

* * *

Harriette Wilson (1789-1846)

Earl of Craven's mistress at fifteen. Most brilliant phase was as mistress of the Duke of Argyll. When she attempted to blackmail the Duke of Wellington by publishing her memoirs, he retorted, 'Publish and be damned'.

All are called virtuous who are supposed to be chaste.

Revenge is sometimes sweet, even to the most forgiving lady.

Without tenderness of heart a woman is unsexed.

The beautiful passion of love! Not that I have known much good resulting from it.

If I have the knack to amuse the public, I shall expect the public to be grateful to me.

Men

'To define a man: he must be a creature who makes me feel that I am a woman.'

Elinor Glyn (1865-1943)

Margot Asquith (1864-1945)

I have always wanted to be a man, if only for the reason that I would like to have gauged the value of my intellect.

*   *   *

Mary Astell (1668-1731)

Man, proud and vain as he is, will lay his boasted authority, the dignity and prerogative of his sex, one moment at her feet; he may call himself her slave a few days, but it is only in order to make her his, all the rest of his life.

Those who go abroad fools, return fops.

On the Beau –

He is one that has more learning in his heels than in his

head. He should be a philosopher, for he studies nothing but himself; yet everyone knows him better, that thinks him not worth knowing.

* * *

Georgianna Anne Bellamy (1731-1788)

The boasted superiority of the men over our sex in the endowments of the mind is a mere commonplace vaunt.

* * *

Marie Bashkirtseff (1860-1884)

In my opinion, to a woman who knows her own mind men can only be a minor consideration.

Men should only be the accessories of the strong woman.

* * *

Saint Catherine of Sienna (1347-1380)

To a brave man, good and bad luck are like his right and left hand. He uses both.

* * *

Margaret Cavendish (1625-1673)

On Fools –

The self-conceited is one that scorns to take council, and not only thinks his fancy the fullest of wit, but that whatsoever is good is created by being his.

The impatient fool is all for the present; for he thinks his throat cut until he is satisfied in his desires.

The learned fool admires and is in love with all other languages beside his own.

The superstitious fool is an observer of times, postures, figures, noises, accidents and dreams. He never enjoys any present recreation for fear of an evil accident.

* * *

Mrs Centlivre (1667-1722)

Concerning the dedication of one of her plays –

I was considering at whose feet to lay the following scenes:

The race of old men presented themselves to my mind, who despising women of their own years, marry girls of fifteen, by which they keep open house for all the young fellows in town, in order to increase their families, and make their tables flourish like the vine: but my aversion to fools of all kinds made me decline them too.

* * *

Christina of Sweden (1626-1689)

You should be more afraid of a stupid man than of an evil one.

Man is not made for pleasure, but pleasure for man.

* * *

Colette (1873-1954)

When a man wants to deceive you, he'll find a way of escape through the tiniest of holes.

The only real masterful noise a man ever makes in a house is that of his key, when he is still on the landing, fumbling for the lock.

* * *

Madame Cornuel (1605-1694)

No man is a hero to his valet.

* * *

Virginia Cowles

Her black list of men –

Men, who take you to a musical comedy, and entertain you by commenting ecstatically on the figures of the chorus.

Men, who tell you how wonderful it is to meet a woman with a mind – then give your hand a squeeze.

Men, who inform you that only men are capable of enduring friendship.

Men, who break off in the middle of a story with a gallant smirk, announcing that the refining presence of a woman does not permit them to continue.

Men, who when rebuffed, inform you that you must be suffering from some strange Freudian complex.

Men, who spend the evening telling how divine you are, then fail to call you up for a week.

Men, who spend the evening telling you how divine someone else is.

* * *

Geneviève Antoine Dariaux

There are three kinds of husbands –

The Blind Man, who at last notices the ensemble you have been wearing for the past two years.

The Ideal Husband, who notices everything. He is extremely rare.

The Dictator, who knows far better than you what is becoming to you.

Men enjoy being envied, but they hate feeling conspicuous. They particularly dislike vulgarity in the women they love.

* * *

THE WIT OF WOMEN

Anne Edwards

Debunking the starry-eyed illusions of a young girl in love –

When your beloved in shining armour gallops up and kills the dragon who was just about to breathe fire all over you – that's folk lore.

When a sheik with passion burning in his eyes gallops up just as you are about to be forced to give your troth to one you don't love, and sweeps you into a saddle and away to love in a tent in the desert – that's film stuff, my child.

If the man who falls in love with you sees some terrible sea monster approaching and immediately plunges a dagger into the monster's shoulder – you can bet your life it's an old classical myth.

The girl who is tied to a stake while Indians dance round emitting fearful war cries and whose lover arrives in the nick of time and shoots them down – it all takes place in a western.

And if you should find yourself lying flat on your back with a crushing machine about to smash you to pulp, and the hero dashes in to save you from a horrible death – it's on the telly.

And when a man says he'd climb the highest mountain, swim the deepest river, or cross the burning desert to find you – it's only a song.

My idea of a screamingly boring man is a chap who doesn't like the company of women.

* * *

MEN

George Eliot (1819-1880)

Blessed is the man who, having nothing to say, abstains from giving wordy evidence of the fact.

I'm not denyin' the women are foolish; God Almighty made them to match the men.

Women know no perfect love: loving the strong, they can forsake the strong; man clings because the being whom he loves is weak and needs him.

Opposition may become sweet to a man, when he has christened it persecution.

Of a conceited man –

He was like a cock, who thought the sun had risen to hear him crow.

An ass may bray a good while before he shakes the stars down.

No man can be wise on an empty stomach.

*   *   *

Queen Elizabeth I (1533-1603)

One man with a head on his shoulders is worth a dozen without.

*   *   *

Penelope Gilliatt

Description of a sycophant –

A good man in the worst sense of the term.

What always makes me laugh is the spectacle of a queer chasing a woman, because he hasn't admitted he's queer. It's like a dog running after a car that has a tin tied on the bumper. Little doggie, what would you do if you caught it?

* * *

Sheilah Graham

Men who are in love are not interested in whether the girl knows an A from a B at the beginning of the relationship. Afterwards they try to improve her.

* * *

Virginia Graham

Men have an instinctive fear of women who talk familiarly about gaskets or isotopes.

* * *

Hedda Hopper (1890-1966)

It's a full-time job holding a man.

* * *

Margery Hurst

Two things I have learned about men. Never compete with them. Never try to change them. To attempt either leads to chaos.

A woman who becomes too much like a man both bores and frightens him.

*   *   *

Angela Ince

Most men, no matter how old, arthritic and peevish, trot through life complacently believing that all women, no matter how young and desirable, are after them.

Life to the average man is a jungle littered with mantraps, wedding rings and tigresses in mini-skirts waiting to pounce. He flits through this jungle, twittering with relief every time he manages to escape (as he thinks) at worst marriage, and at best an expensive dinner.

A calming thought for men –

Take refuge in statistics. There are more of you than us, these days. We're not chasing any more, we're choosing.

*   *   *

Mary Wilson Little

If a man is only a little lower than the angels, the angels should reform.

* * *

Anita Loos

Gentlemen prefer blondes, but they marry brunettes.

Gentlemen always seem to remember blondes.

Through Lorelei, heroine of 'Gentlemen Prefer Blondes':

I really think that American gentlemen are the best after all, because kissing your hand may make you feel very good, but a diamond and sapphire bracelet lasts forever.

Every time a French gentlemen starts in to squeal, you can always stop him with five francs, no matter who he is.

Spending money is only just a habit, and if you get a gentleman started on buying one dozen orchids at a time, he really gets very good habits.

When a girl really enjoys being with a gentleman, it puts her to quite a disadvantage, and no real good can come of it.

A girl with brains ought to do something else with them besides think.

Clare Boothe Luce

Time comes when every man's got to feel something new – when he's got to feel young again, just because he's growing old.

There's nothing like a good dose of another woman to make a man appreciate his wife.

* * *

Jayne Mansfield (1933-1967)

Men are those creatures with two legs and eight hands.

* * *

'Ouida' (1839-1908)

Opposition to man in love is like oil to fire.

Women hope that the dead love may revive; but men know that of all dead things none is so past recall as a dead passion.

* * *

Marjorie Proops

Nine out of ten women would rather have a man who would surreptitiously caress their thighs under a nightclub table than a good, rugged chap who'll slap them heartily on the back at a Saturday football game.

If there's a worse insult I don't know it. I have just been told by my friend Gladys that she'd trust her husband to spend an evening alone with me.

Everyone, wherever you go, is in *conference* these days.

* * *

Helen Rowland (1875-1950)

A bachelor never quite gets over the idea that he is a thing of beauty and a boy forever.

The follies which a man regrets most in his life are those which he didn't commit when he had the opportunity.

A husband is what is left of the lover after the nerve has been extracted.

It's as hard to get a man to stay at home after you've married him, as it was to get him to go home before you married him.

It takes a woman twenty years to make a man of her son, and another woman twenty minutes to make a fool of him.

Never trust a husband too far, or a bachelor too near.

To a woman the first kiss is the end of the beginning; to a man it is the beginning of the end.

One man's folly is another man's wife.

A woman need know but one man well, in order to understand all men; whereas a man may know all women and understand not one of them.

A bachelor who has passed forty is a remnant; there is no good material in him.

A man always asks for 'Just one kiss' – because he knows that if he can get that, the rest will come without asking.

* * *

George Sand (1804-1876)

Woe to the man who tries to be frank in love-making.

* * *

Madeleine de Scudéry (1607-1701)

Men should keep their eyes wide open before marriage, and half shut afterwards.

* * *

Madame de Sévigné (1626-1696)

I fear nothing so much as a man who is witty all day long.

*   *   *

Rebecca West, DBE

The trouble about man is twofold. He cannot learn truths which are too complicated; he forgets truths which are too simple.

Politics

'The world grows older but not wiser; women and Parliaments still trust the same sort of men who have continually deceived them.'
Lady of Fashion, 1780

Baroness Asquith, DBE (1887-1969)

On the occasion (1967) when women were invited for the first time to the Royal Academy dinner.

This is indeed an historic occasion – for it makes the end of *purdah* for this great monastic fellowship. For the first time in its long and glorious history, the Royal Academy of Arts – sometimes accused of hidebound orthodoxy – has flung tradition to the winds, confounded all its critics and detractors, by a daring and almost reckless experiment. They have actually invited women out to dinner!

But that is not all – women are not merely to be seen here tonight (for what that is worth – rather an overrated treat, I have always thought), but they are actually to be heard as well. To me – how undeservedly – has fallen the honour of being the first to break the sound barrier. Would that I were more supersonic! Would that I could do it with a bang! At least, I promise to avoid a whimper.

On Lloyd George –

He couldn't see a belt without hitting below it.

* * *

Lady Nancy Astor (1879-1964)

A heckler at a political meeting: Say, Missus, how many toes are there on a pig's foot?
Lady Astor: Take off your boots, man, and count for yourself.

The Welfare State may be the Farewell State.

Sir Stafford Cripps has a brilliant mind until it is made up.

From her maiden speech in the House of Commons –

Drink really promises you everything and gives you nothing.

Women are young at politics, but they are old at suffering.

* * *

Nancy Boyd (1892-1950)

He is a politician. He has spent the best years of his life in an endeavour to make the world safe for stupidity.

* * *

E M Braddock, MP

Boxers are not dragged into the ring, although they might sometimes be dragged out. They go voluntarily.

Commenting on her size –

People believe that I am such a hefty individual that, wherever I go, they come to see whether I am really as big as I have been made out to be. To me that has been useful indeed.

* * *

Baroness Burton

A woman in authority is often unpopular, only because she is efficient.

If you get a good woman, you get the finest thing on earth.

* * *

Joyce Butler, MP

To the Prime Minister –

Women are fed up with being exploited as pretty birds when young, and silly moos when they get older – as a substitute for equal human rights now.

* * *

Catherine the Great (1729-1796)

Power without a nation's confidence is nothing.

Peace is necessary to this vast empire. We need population, not devastation.

Polygamy is useful for the purpose of population.

There is no need to forbid young men to travel for fear they may abscond, if we make their native country attractive to them.

* * *

Baroness Elliot, DBE

The days of political speeches as such are over – particularly when you are talking to women. They are rarely carried away by them.

* * *

POLITICS

Winifred Ewing, MP

The English are the greatest nationalists in the world, but they're also the subtlest. They do it by convincing everyone that any other kind of nationalism is in bad taste, and they've somehow put it across.

You have to wrap everything up in cotton wool when you are dealing with a man, and flatter him up to the eyebrows. You can deal directly and honestly with a woman. We are the realistic sex.

From a speech to the Scottish National Party –

You have put me in the best seat in the stalls of what is really the best show in the West End. The trouble, for Scotland, is that there is always the same play showing, and it is called *A Comedy of Errors*.

*   *   *

Baroness Gaitskell

On the House of Lords Debate on Homosexuality –

Some people regard sex between a man and a woman as between a man and a plastic model of Brigitte Bardot – hermetically sealed.

*   *   *

Baroness Horsbrugh, GBE

Let's look after our tempers, as we look after our stockings.

* * *

Lena Jeger, MP

On the new Divorce Bill –

The law can put only certain limitations on human behaviour. It cannot make a man loyal or a woman loving.

* * *

The Rt Hon Jennie Lee, PC, MP

On being elected an MP –

I simply could not understand why what I looked like, what I wore, my favourite breakfast, and whether I thought whiskers should be curled upwards or downwards, had anything to do with the serious political purposes that engaged my working hours.

* * *

Joan Lestor, MP

On the 'Divorce by Consent' Bill –

Casanovas have never needed a charter to be Casanovas.

They have done it within the existing law. I do not believe that large numbers of men in this country wish to desert their wives, or wish to break up the marriage home.

Nor do I accept the argument that women would be deserted in favour of younger and fresher ladies. Very often it seems to me that middle-aged gentlemen overrate the attraction they have for younger women.

* * *

Elsa Maxwell (1883-1963)

To the interpreter at a Khrushchev reception –

Tell the Premier that for a party of mine, no one needs to carry a card. Just an invitation.

* * *

Baroness Phillips

I like to have a real enemy to fight. It gives me something I can get my teeth into.

Is it too much to ask that the housewife be trained for a shopping spree?

* * *

George Sand (1804-1876)

Party politics is now a real farce.

* * *

Baroness Stocks

Morality – we don't call it sin today, we call it self-expression.

There has always been the Bright Young Thing. She is feathery-headed, and in different generations expresses herself in different ways. But essentially she doesn't change. With the aid of wealth and leisure she will always flourish.

* * *

The Rt Hon Baroness Summerskill, PC, CH

The first man to cause a strike against the exploitation of women workers will indeed be the pin-up boy of women in industry.

There is nothing that changes a woman's affection for a man into indifference more quickly than the realisation that the husband holds the purse strings too tightly, and that she is forced into the humiliating position of asking for every penny she needs.

My advice to any girl anxious to explore the world outside her home after marriage, is to choose a man not only intelligent and capable, but above all one who is able to cook a light meal without regarding it as a slur on his virility.

* * *

Queen Victoria (1819-1901)

Referring to Gladstone –

He speaks to ME, as if I were a public meeting.

* * *

Ellen Wilkinson (1891-1947)

Led the famous march of the unemployed from her constituency, Jarrow, to London.

I found out what a difference a white tablecloth and a paper serviette can make to one's outlook on life.

* * *

Baroness Wootton

Too much 'anti-ness' on the Left threatens attainment of that better-ordered world most of us say we'd like to see.

Food

'Forget about the experts, it's the look on the guests' faces which really counts.'
                                        Madeleine Bingham

Eliza Acton (1799-1859)

Eat, to live.

Good cookery is the best and truest economy.

*   *   *

Madeleine Bingham

Beauty is in the eye and mind of the eater. Even if the salmon has been dropped on the lino, it's come up smiling. Let the guests remain in equally smiling ignorance.

Cooking, like unrequited love, is all in the mind. Once a girl has decided her ex-boy-friend is a fat slob, she can forget all about him. It is just the same with burned cakes.

Too many cooks may spoil the broth, but it only takes one to burn it.

There may be as many good fish in the sea as ever came out of it, but cooking them is even more difficult than catching them.

I have never found in cookery books the things which actually happen to me. The cookery book writers never spill oil on the floor, slip on it and bring a bowl of mayonnaise crashing to the ground, breaking the lot, with a dinner party arriving in half-an-hour, and not a shop in sight.... Does it matter what finally gets to the table so long as the guests can eat it? I've always thought Alfred showed a marked lack of ingenuity over cakes – why didn't he cut off the burned bits, and ice the rest?

* * *

Brigid Brophy

Vegetarians will query the Good Shepherd as a symbol of tenderness towards his flock, since he may well be preserving his sheep from being eaten by a wolf in order to make sure they shall presently be eaten by men.

* * *

Cleopatra

After Mark Antony had done his utmost to entertain Cleopatra, feasting her day by day, sparing no cost, she began to debase the expense of his fare.

When he demanded to know how it was possible to go beyond

this magnificence, she answered that she would spend, on one supper for him, ten million sesterii (twenty million pence). Antony, believing this impossible, laid a great wager with her about it.

The sumptuous Royal supper was laid, but Antony laughed Cleopatra to scorn, asking to see the bill for each item. Cleopatra affirmed that, not only would she keep her promise, but that the supper would cost sixty million sesterii. With that, she commanded the second course to be brought in. A servant entered, and placed before her a goblet of a sharp and special vinegar, the strength of which was even able to dissolve pearls. Now Cleopatra was wearing as earrings two most precious pearls in the world. As Antony looked wistfully at her, wondering what she would do, she took off one earring, dropped it into the vinegar and, as soon as it was liquefied, drank it off. She was about to do the same with the other earring, but Plancus, the judge of the wager, caught her hand, and pronounced that a furious Antony had lost the wager. It was then that Cleopatra murmured to her lover –

No soldier is a match for a woman.

* * *

Madame du Barry (1741-1793)

How she outwitted Louis XV.

Louis XV of France always professed loudly that it was impossible for any woman to attain the peak of perfection in the culinary art.

This piqued his mistress, Madame du Barry, who invited

the King to a supper made by the best 'cuisinière' in France.

The royal voluptuary was enraptured, and asked, 'Who is this new "cuisinier" of yours? He must join the Royal Household.'

'It is no "cuisinier", it is a "cuisinière", and I demand a recompense worthy both of her and Your Majesty. I cannot accept less than a Cordon Bleu for her.'

And that is how the famous honour became part of Cookery.

* * *

Maria Floris (1892-1967)

Cooking is a serious matter, but it should also be fun.

The English language is full of pitfalls. I have never understood the meaning of the word 'offal'. I always thought it was stuff one put in the dustbin.

Nobody can cook as well as mother.

The English breakfast is the best and cleverest in the world. It is a real meal and fortifies you for the whole day.

On cooking –

The skill you acquire is far more important than the housekeeping budget with which you have to work.

Whatever else you put in your recipe, you must put your heart into it. Your heart is by far the most important ingredient.

* * *

Virginia Graham

Tea-time –

> May every tea-time be accursed,
> May honey spill and éclairs burst,
> And may those ladies die of thirst
> Who dare to put the milk in first!

* * *

Madame Prunier

If a woman is intelligent and hard working, she can equal a man.

I always mix business with pleasure.

If you are a Frenchwoman, you must justify the fact.

I think the wisest thing, if you are a woman in business, is to stay feminine, no matter what kind of brain you may have.

* * *

Elsa Schiaparelli

A good cook is like a sorceress who dispenses happiness.

*   *   *

Edith Sitwell, DBE (1887-1964)

On English cooking –

The cooking of vegetables! Each vegetable as much an island as our beloved England, but set, not in silver seas, but in the salt sea; each meal the kind which might have been served up by avenging angels at dinner parties in the Cities of Plain – deserts of sand, pillars of salt, wine made from Dead Sea fruit.

Beauty and Fashion

> 'There are no ugly women, only lazy ones.'
> Helena Rubinstein (1882–1965)

Elizabeth Arden (1891-1966)

On the Beauty business –

I think this is the nastiest business in the world. There are so many people in it, and they all just copy me.

I'm not interested in age. People who tell their age are silly. You're as young as you feel.

Working towards beauty is plain horse sense.

It is high time that women became women again. It is high time that women became glamorous, inspiring creatures again. It is psychologically impossible for the woman, who looks like a sheared, shorn male, to think, or feel, or fascinate like a female.

* * *

BEAUTY AND FASHION

Bettina Ballard (1903-1961)

The fashion world is akin to the political world – a good place in which to exert power, influence people, and give expression to the ego.

The fashion world is no place for the timid, dedicated souls; it is a field for strong determined egoists, who have an innate desire to impose their will on the world – wills of iron disguised in rustling silks and beautiful colours.

We in America accept fashion the way we accept electricity – as something we can turn on and off, and that is always available.

* * *

Ernestine Carter

Nostalgia for quality is raising its nose above the sea of shoddy. After all, even whizz-kids can't stop the clock, and wonder-boys become men, sometimes not so wonderful. And what is a sadder thought than a middle-aged hippie?

* * *

Gabrielle 'Coco' Chanel

On the modern fashion –

Wearing a skirt halfway up the thigh does not give woman an advantage. Fashion should not come up from the street.

On Male Couturiers –

Those who do not like women should have nothing to do with them, because their only intention is to make them look ridiculous.

An enormous world of fashion has grown up which lives on stupidity. Their so-called sophistication is such that it is becoming almost shameful to dress women as women.

* * *

Agatha Christie

Commenting on Dress –

Life nowadays is dominated and complicated by the remorseless Zip. Is there anything more deadly than a Zip that turns nasty on you?

* * *

Geneviève Antoine Dariaux

A grandmother disguised as Brigitte Bardot is no more ridiculous than a teenager masquerading in an outfit suitable for a worldly woman of forty.

It is a good rule never to go shopping with a girl-friend. She will unconsciously demolish everything that suits you best. Shop alone, and only telephone the next day to make a date with your best girl-friend.

* * *

Prudence Glynn

There is a joke around London that you can only tell the girls from the boys, because the boys have moustaches. However deplorable you may find the idea, the fact is that the once obvious distinction between the sexes becomes more blurred every day.

In times of threat to our sex, women automatically adopt a style of dress most likely to avoid undesirability – that fate which to most of us is so infinitely worse than death.

Luckily, in the fashion world no one expects a perfect knowledge of geography or history, and so a great deal of latitude is permitted to clothes.

On watching Paris fashion shows –

You don't become a cliché for nothing. Distance does lend enchantment even to a jaundiced view, time does heal the scars left by neighbours' elbows, inadequate seating, and the hotel bill.

That much publicised moth, the permissive attitude, has riddled the wardrobe as diligently as it has eaten holes in our moral clothing.

* * *

THE WIT OF WOMEN

Felicity Green

Commenting on Royal Ascot –

The clothes that this week will be gracing the racing scene, have about as much to do with fashion as a chimpanzee's tea-party has with a Lord Mayor's Banquet. . . . Here and there among the gimmicks and the ghastlies are some perfectly well-dressed women. But it needs an expert form-spotter to find them among what appears to be the entire cast of a second-rate touring company of the Ziegfeld Follies.

It's touching the way the Strong Sex always worry about the Fair Sex. . . . Apart from the food we eat, the clothes we wear also menace our well-being. When you think about all these hazards, it's funny to remember that woman's expectancy of life is now eight years longer than man's.

On Fashion –

There is no sign of a return to what was fondly known as normal in the day when women were women – Gad, sir, only Hamlet wore a doublet and hose, and long socks were for Boy Scouts!

*   *   *

Hedda Hopper (1890-1966)

Famous for her hats –

I can wear a hat or take it off, but either way it's a conversation piece.

* * *

Mary Wilson Little

Beauty in a woman's face, like sweetness in a woman's lips, is a matter of taste.

* * *

Mary Quant

Once only the rich set the fashion. Now it is the inexpensive little dress seen on the girls in the High Street.

Since the sexes live much the same sort of lives, they want the same sort of clothes to live them in.

All women, whether they go to work in a bus or a Bentley, worry about what to wear.

A fashionable woman wears clothes. The clothes don't wear her.

Fashion is not frivolous. It is part of being alive today.

Sex appeal has absolutely Number One priority.

A woman is as young as her knee.

I don't believe that happiness is a lost art; I don't believe it is an art at all. It is simply that the accepted symbols of happiness have changed. In the nineteenth century, a woman accepted her lot as a happy one if . .
> She had a husband who didn't beat her every day.
> Her children were a credit to her.
> She was allowed to join in the conversation at dinner – at least until the port arrived and the talk became interesting.

Now – it would seem – for a woman to be happy, she must have . . .
> A career . . . a spin dryer . . . diamonds . . . TV . . . a mink-lined mackintosh . . . a lover . . . an electric toaster . . . good health . . . pep-pills . . . and sedatives . . . two cars (at least) . . . Jane Fonda's face and Simone de Beauvoir's intellect . . . a working knowledge of child psychology . . . a child . . . a husband who beats her every Friday.

*   *   *

Helena Rubinstein (1882-1965)

I have always felt that a woman has the right to treat the subject of her age with ambiguity until, perhaps, she passes into the realm of over ninety. Then it is better she be candid with herself and with the world.

Hard work keeps the wrinkles out of the mind and spirit.

Why is it so easy to persuade a pretty woman to do something more for herself, but so hard to start a plain woman doing anything?

Plain women have been made to feel that beauties are made in heaven and not actually on earth, as, of course, they are.

*   *   *

Elsa Schiaparelli

Many men admire strong women, but they do not love them. Some women have achieved a combination of strength and tenderness, but most of those who have wanted to walk alone have, in the course of the game, lost their happiness.

A dress cannot just hang like a painting on a wall, or, like a book, remain intact and live a long and sheltered life. A dress has no life of its own unless it is worn, and as soon as this happens, another personality takes over from you and animates it, or tries to, glorifies or destroys it, or makes it into a song of beauty.

The moment that people stop copying you, it means that you are no longer any good, and that you have ceased to be news.

*   *   *

Edith Sitwell (1887-1964)

The Englishwoman's clothes have improved out of all knowledge. No longer are our hats, as in Victorian days, a kind of Pageant of Empire, whereon the products of all the colonies battle for precedence.

* * *

Elsie de Wolfe (?1858-1950)

Do not mistake eccentricity for chic. They have not even a bowing acquaintance.

Stage and Screen

'A good actress lasts, and sex attraction does not.'
Brigitte Bardot

Sophie Arnould (1744-1802)

Women give themselves to God when the Devil wants nothing more to do with them.

People have grown so rude these days, that they call things by their right names.

A woman, whose favours a man seeks, is like an enigma of which people are eager to find the solution; no sooner is the secret known than all interest ceases.

Of the Controller-General of Finances, who suffered from cold hands –

That's strange, since he always has them in other people's pockets.

On meeting a physician armed with a gun –

Are you afraid that your prescriptions will not be sufficient?

To an actress who complained that it was terrible to be so near her fortieth birthday –

Take courage, my dear, and be consoled with the reflection that every day takes you farther away from it.

The heart of a flirt is a rose. Each lover bears away a leaf. The thorns are left for the husband.

*   *   *

Tallulah Bankhead (1903-1968)

Once described herself as 'Pure as the driven slush'.
Asked in recent years 'Are you really Tallulah Bankhead?' she replied –

What's left of her, dahling.

Her criticism of a pretentious play –

There is less in this than meets the eye.

America is my family, England is my lover.

When she was fifty-four –

They used to shoot Shirley Temple through gauze. You ought to shoot me through linoleum.

I read Shakespeare and the Bible, and I can shoot dice. That's what I call a liberal education.

The only thing I regret about my past is the length of it. If I had to live my life again I'd make all the same mistakes – only sooner.

I have only two temperamental outbursts a year – each lasts six months.

Whatever you have read I have said is almost certainly untrue, except if it is funny, in which case I definitely said it.

*   *   *

Brigitte Bardot

Love is the most important thing in my life. Without it, I cannot survive. After love, way, way down, comes everything else.

I have a big appetite for life.

If you live with a man you must conquer him every day. Otherwise he will go to another.

I have absolutely no ambition. I just want to live, and be happy.

* * *

Sarah Bernhardt (1844-1923)

Legend remains victorious in spite of history.

It is truly strange that man's mind should have made of life a perpetual strife.

When an Englishman opens his door to you, he never closes it again.

When advised to slow down –

Slow down? Rest? With all eternity before me?

The actress, Madge Kendal, congratulating the 'Divine Sarah' on her performance, added that it was a pity that her plays dealt with passion, so that she could not take her daughters to see them – to which Bernhardt replied –

Ah, Madame, you should remember that were it not for passion, you would have no daughters to bring.

* * *

STAGE AND SCREEN

Caryl Brahms

Criticising Desdemona in 'Othello' –

She seemed a dull girl, interested only in sex. I was reminded of an exchange from an American kitchen-sink play:

Married daughter to her husband (for the third time):	Come to bed, Sammy.
Father (exasperated):	What's so special about bed?

On Charles Laughton's King Lear –

A ruined King? Rather the wreck of a man who has built his all on backing the outsider that failed to win the Selling-plate.

I feel about laughter what the coloured girl felt about an orgy – it ain't no good ignoring it – you just gotta join in.

On a ballet performance –

Carmen Amaya, a Spanish dancer, is making her first appearance supported by her relatives; and upon reflection I daresay they do at least as well as yours or mine might have done in the circumstances.

*   *   *

Mrs Patrick Campbell (1865-1940)

To a journalist who remarked on her coldness to his profession –

There is only one complaint I ever make. They will call me 'Mrs Pat'. I can't stand it. The 'Pat' is the last straw that breaks the Campbell's back.

Many people say that I have an ugly mind. It isn't true. I say ugly things, which is different.

* * *

Jackie Collins

I like men to know what they're at, if you know what I mean.

I think acting is the biggest drag of all time for a girl.

Some American producers discuss actresses as if they were a load of cows.

* * *

Bette Davis

I'm a ham, that is a good ham. A good ham is an actor who really enjoys giving pleasure to people.

I used to hate my face when I was young, and now I'm

glad. It's a blessing. But I never kidded myself into thinking the crap I made was really art in disguise.

But all that is over now. I'm not rich, but I don't need money as much now as I used to, so I no longer need to make crap.

Speaking of her five marriages –

I am a woman meant for a man, but I never found a man who could compete.

* * *

Marlene Dietrich

Jealousy, an uncontrollable passion. The Siamese twin of love.

The lover's criterion is: I want you to be happy – but with me.

Don't follow fashion blindly into every dark alley. Always remember that you are not a model or a mannequin for which the fashion is created.

* * *

Marie Dressler (1869-1934)

If ants are such busy workers, how come they find time to go to all the picnics?

A rut is like a grave – it's only a question of depth.

*   *   *

Isadora Duncan (1878-1927)

After a successful dance performance –

It would be much kinder if they sent me champagne while I am alive; they can send me flowers when I am dead.

On America (having come from Russia) –

If I had come to this country as a great financier to borrow money, I would have been given a great reception, but as I came as a recognised artist, I was sent to Ellis Island as a dangerous character.

*   *   *

Eleonora Duse (1859-1924)

When we grow old, there can only be one regret – not to have given enough of ourselves.

The sensible man and the silent woman are the best conversation.

To be often in love shows a frivolous mind, but to be never in love shows a stupid one.

STAGE AND SCREEN

Women, instead of trying to conquer on the field, urged on by war-like instincts, pushing themselves into business, journalism, and even commerce, should remember that independence is grand, but that mixing in affairs makes them eventually lose the gentleness and sweetness that is the one thing given them to hold man's devotion.

There are times when there is nothing more humiliating in life than the knowledge of being inferior to one's reputation.

I have the greatest of all riches: that of not desiring them.

No famous man or woman, least of all an actress, should ever write their memoirs; or if they did, they should wait until the age of earthly jealousy has passed.

After Sarah Bernhardt had venomously criticised Duse –

Tell Madame Bernhardt that I am not writing my memoirs, nor have I any intention of writing them; but that she had better pray to God that I never change my mind.

* * *

Gracie Fields

When people retire they sort of die, so I reckon I'll enjoy myself while I can.

I don't care what's going to happen to me tomorrow. I just want to get on with what's happening today.

THE WIT OF WOMEN

A tip to the overnight teenage stars –

Getting big money? Save it, love, while they're paying out.

Money never buys happiness for grownups, only for kids. They're the only people that money can buy happiness for.

* * *

Mary Garden (1877-1967)

Don't lean on anyone but yourself.

What people said when a perfume, Gardenia, was named after her –

'Oh, there's the lady of the perfume!' I was never the lady who sang!

During the shooting of Samuel Goldwyn's film production of 'Thaïs', in which Mary Garden starred –

The gentleman putting it on knew nothing about Egypt and had no intention of finding out. I was supposed to be walking in the garden, and along my path were thirty parrots on their perches.
'Scratch their heads!' the director shouted at me.
'You're not serious,' I protested.

'Scratch their heads!' he demanded.
'All of them?' I asked.
'Each and every one of them!'

And scratch their heads I did. For a hundred and twenty-five thousand dollars I suppose I would have scratched the heads of all the parrots in the world.

* * *

Hermione Gingold

I like to know what a picture represents without being told by the artist. Ladies with no mouth and six arms; gentlemen with eyes in their stomachs and legs of grand pianos; landscapes with wardrobe trunks overflowing with human limbs and peopled by alarm clocks with black silk-stockinged feet, only make me laugh, and anyone who can take them seriously has my dying admiration.

Advice to an 'Ex-Millionairess' –

No matter how old they are do not throw your diamonds away. You will find they can still be used for many purposes, such as scratching your initials on glass.

I got all the schooling any actress needs. That is, I learned to write well enough to sign contracts.

* * *

Joyce Grenfell

All human faces are divided into buttons, birds and horses.

Obituary on a woman who died listening to a difficult piece of modern music –

She died of opening her mind too wide.

*   *   *

Yvette Guilbert (1865-1944)

Furious because of savage criticism by the redoubtable critic, Sarcey, she forced her way into his study –

'You are an insolent cad, who makes cowardly attacks on a woman.'
'I regret,' said Mr Sarcey, waving his hand towards the pile of papers on his desk, 'that pile of white sheets must be covered before noon, and if we have no more to say to each other . . .'

The raging Yvette seized the brass inkstand and, in a flash, overturned it on the sheets –

'They were to be dirtied. They are dirtied.'

One cannot remain the same. Art is a mirror which

should show many reflections, and the artist should not always show the same face, or the face becomes a mask.

*   *   *

Helen Hayes

Commenting on a theatre named after her –

An actress's life is so transitory. Suddenly you're a building!

*   *   *

Katharine Hepburn

Because of her contempt for publicity, once ungenerously labelled 'Katharine of Arrogance' –

If you survive long enough, you're revered rather like an old building.

No nice man should marry an actress, or anyone else whose mind is always on herself. If I were a man, I wouldn't be dumb enough to marry someone who couldn't pass a mirror without looking in it.

There comes a time in your life when people get very sweet to you – I think they're beginning to think I'm not going to be around much longer.

*   *   *

Anne Heywood

In America, if you're demure, they think you are just dumb.

* * *

Josephine Hull

Playing Shakespeare is very tiring. You never get to sit down, unless you're a King.

* * *

Elsie Janis (1889-1968)

I have never been really virtuous. I have only been egotistical.

My epitaph – 'Here lies Elsie Janis, still sleeping alone!'

* * *

Eartha Kitt

You don't have to hit anybody on the head with four-letter words to be sexy.

Title of her new book –

A Tart is not a Sweet.

* * *

Elsa Lanchester (Mrs Charles Laughton)

If I can't be a good artist without too much pain, then I'm damned if I'll be an artist at all.

Comedians on the stage are invariably suicidal when they get home.

One thinks of a film star as a kind of gaily coloured bird, forever giving itself a final preening under the bright lights. Whereas it's all hard work, aspirins and usually purgatives.

To complain too bitterly of the load of mischief that notoriety brings with it would mean that you are unsuited to the position you made for yourself.

Every artist should be allowed a few failures.

A woman can absorb the same beauty hint at least twice a week provided it keeps that flag of hope flying.

A woman should look upon her own face every morning as an artist's canvas, and in this case the better the painter the greater the economy of line and the thinner the paint.

* * *

Vivien Leigh (1913-1967)

I can't add two and two together. I don't know whether I'm a wealthy woman or not. How *can* one be in this country, if one's an artist?

Most of us have compromised with life. Those who fight for what they want will always thrill us.

*   *   *

Caroline Lejeune

From reviews of films –

There are snake dances, sacrifices, private swimming baths, a Holy Mountain. The Mountain, by the way, has the privilege of belching when it is dissatisfied, something that the well-bred critic must not do.

All the best whimsy puts sardines above caviar, sees heaven in a bed-sitting room, and stars in a puddle.

> Cecil B de Mille
> Much against his will,
> Was persuaded to leave Moses
> Out of the Wars of the Roses.

Review of the film 'I Am A Camera' –

Me no leica.

Sometimes I think that the human race has a very poor discrimination in regard to its great men. It's all very well to put up a statue to a man who won a battle, but what about a plaque, just a simple one, to the man who ate the first oyster or the man who invented the zip fastener.

Her comment on a film actor –

> I always think of Sonny Tufts
> As something very large from Crufts.

*　　*　　*

Beatrice Lillie (Lady Peel)

I'm a LADY in my own wrong.

When asked whether she had performed during the First World War, she answered –

At the *end* of the First World War – when I was knee-high to a hiccup!

While enjoying a typically glittering dinner and 'evening' at Buckingham Palace, Miss Lillie turned what, to most people, would have been an unpleasant and embarrassing incident, into unforgettable hilarity, when in reaction to the spilling of a serving spoon of steaming soup down her evening gown, she drew herself up instantly in mock horror and delivered this gem to the apologising, shaken Palace waiter –

Never darken my DIOR again!

Beatrice Lillie was seated at her desk in her flat in New York, dealing with her correspondence, when a pigeon flew through the window and perched on a chair. Without turning a hair, Miss Lillie addressed the bird –

Any messages?

One recent Saint Patrick's Day in New York City, Miss Lillie embarked in a taxi on the East Side to go the to West Side. The taxi had to cross Fifth Avenue, which was cordoned off for most of its length, and down which the proud Irish followed the long green stripe painted for the occasion. The journey was finally accomplished after a circuitous and hectic ride, and by an extremely bad-tempered driver. Having endured his 'blather' and bad driving, Miss Lillie finished him off, while giving him a nominal tip –

Something for you, driver – buy yourself a sense of humour.

Some years ago Miss Lillie, carrying her Pekinese puppy, hailed a taxi for a lengthy ride to the Savoy Hotel. In giving Miss Lillie change, the driver glanced into the cab and, to his dismay, he saw that the puppy had misbehaved on the seat. As he started to complain vehemently, the Savoy doorman whipped open the door of the cab and, as she alighted, Lady Peel, giving the driver a handsome gratuity, silenced him forever with –

I did it.

When Miss Lillie came to her hair appointment in a Chicago Beauty Salon, she found that many members of her company were also being processed. As she neared completion, she heard a snooty, affected female voice over the partition say: 'Oh! If I'd known there would be all these theatrical people here today, I would NEVER have come.' The woman was prevailed upon to wait a few minutes. Miss Lillie asked who the woman was, and learned that she was Mrs Armour, wife of the famous meat-packing tycoon. Ready to leave, after a suitable period, an exquisitely dressed and groomed Beatrice Lillie appeared in the waiting room – never looked at her victim – and bid adieu to the manageress with –

'You may tell the butcher's wife that Lady Peel has finished.'

At a social gathering, Beatrice Lillie was wearing a row of pearls which excited the envy and attention of a guest –

'Are they real?' she asked.
'Of course,' replied Miss Lillie.
The woman grabbed the pearls and tried to bite them. 'They're not,' she said, 'they're cultured.'
Miss Lillie smiled sadly and said, 'How would you know – with false teeth!'

*   *   *

Marie Lloyd (1870-1922)

On her fortieth birthday –

I'm forty and no woman knows what falling in love can mean until she's forty.

You could cover a sow's ear with silk purses, and the damn bristles would still work through.

Title of one of her famous songs –

A little of what you fancy does yer good.

No woman cares about being a toff or a real lady – every one of them wants to be told they look heavenly.

*   *   *

Carole Lombard (1909-1942)

Anybody in Hollywood who has her appendix and tonsils is a doctor.

Hollywood is where they write the alibis before they write the story.

*   *   *

Blanche Marchesi (1863-1940)

Advice to temperamental would-be stars –

Nobody is absolutely necessary; everybody can be replaced in this world at a minute's notice. While one great man is climbing the hills of fame, his successor is already born, and when he descends the other side, the successor will be at the top of the hill.

But this simple truth is never believed, every man hoping that he will form an exception to the rule.

* * *

Adah Isaacs Menken (1835-1868)

The famous 'Mazeppa', clad in pink silk fleshings, strapped to the back of a 'fiery steed', known as the 'Naked Lady'. Mistress of Alexandre Dumas père, and of the poet, Swinburne.

You know what Hell is said to be paved with. I believe that I am a very large shareholder in the pavement.

People always find me out, and then find fault with God because I have gifts denied to them.

* * *

Marilyn Monroe (1926-1962)

'Didn't you have anything on?' asked a journalist about her nude picture –

Oh yes, I had the radio on.

Asked what she thought of sex –

It's part of nature and I go along with nature. I don't believe in false modesty. A woman only hurts herself that way.

TV sets should be taken out of the bedroom.

Asked about her famous wiggle –

I learned to walk as a baby, and I haven't had a lesson since.

'What do you wear in bed?' she was asked.
'Chanel Number Five,' she answered.

*   *   *

Mary Pickford

While I would have not missed that Yesterday, I have no desire to go back and live it over. For me now, there is only the great Today, and the promise of Tomorrow.

I was talked into making *The Taming of the Shrew* against my better judgment. Instead of being a forceful tiger cat, I was a spitting little kitten.

* * *

Rachel (Elisa Felix) (1821-1858)

On being congratulated by Count Mole on having saved the French language, she replied –

Good for me, since I never learned it!

It is the business of a woman to answer questions rather than to ask them.

If I marry, goodbye to the actress, and in her place only one married woman the more!

It is better to be abused by the Press than ignored.

The public and the world consider only the artist, they forget the woman.

* * *

Ginger Rogers

The only way to enjoy anything in this life is to earn it first.

I live for today, that's why people think I'm strange. I don't even have a psychiatrist.

* * *

Rosalind Russell

Success is a public affair. Failure is a private funeral.

* * *

Elizabeth Taylor

Beauty? Who wants it? I want a home in a quiet place, where no one knows my name, except the grocer, the butcher, and the milk roundsman.

I think I've licked life at every level.

I just want to be *alive*. I don't want to be a puppet any more. That's why I talk of retiring.

Speaking of her husband Richard Burton –

We want more time together to enjoy life. We still know how to, thank God – we're absolutely unblasé about what we have.

When people say: she's got everything, I've only one answer: I haven't had tomorrow.

* * *

Sophie Tucker (1884-1966)

No man ever put up with a successful woman, and he's right.

The closer you get to vice, the less gilt and glamour you find there is to it.

I have been poor and I have been rich. Rich is better.

The poor know their relatives much better than the rich do.

* * *

Mae West

I'm never vulgar. I kid sex. I take it out in the open and laugh at it.

I used to be Snow White, but I drifted.

It's not the men in my life, but the life in my men that counts.

The best way to hold a man is in your arms.

Love conquers all things except poverty and toothache.

Acknowledgments

We have made every effort to trace the ownership of copyrighted quotations. If we have innocently erred, we express our regret. Thanks and acknowledgments are due to the following:

Polly Adler, *A House is not a Home* – the Estate of the late Polly Adler, and Wm Heinemann.

Margot Asquith, *More Memoirs*, Eyre & Spottiswoode, edited by – Mark Bonham-Carter; *The Autobiography of Margot Asquith* – Thornton Butterworth.

Bettina Ballard, *In My Fashion* – Secker & Warburg.

Madeleine Bingham, *The Bad Cook's Guide* – Corgi Mini Books.

Nancy Boyd (pseudonym of Edna St Vincent Millay), *Distressing Dialogues* – Harper & Row, © 1924, 1951 by Edna St Vincent Millay and Norma Millay Ellis. 'First Fig' from *Collected Poems* – Harper & Row, © 1922, 1950 by Edna St Vincent Millay, by permission of Norma Millay Ellis.

Caryl Brahms, *No Castanets: The Rest of the Evening's My Own* – W H Allen.

Barbara Cartland, *Husbands and Wives* – Arthur Barker.

Ilka Chase, *Free Admission* – © 1948 by Ilka Chase, reprinted by permission of Doubleday & Co. Inc.

Agatha Christie, *Come, Tell Me How You Live* – Collins;

ACKNOWLEDGMENTS

Witness for the Prosecution – Samuel French.

Lady Diana Cooper, *Trumpets from the Steep* – Rupert Hart-Davis.

Geneviève Antoine Dariaux, *Elegance* and *The Men in My Life* – Frederick Muller.

Margaret Drabble, *The Millstone* – Weidenfeld & Nicolson.

Edna Ferber, reprinted by permission of the Estate of Edna Ferber, all rights reserved.

Maria Floris, *Cooking for Love* – Christopher Floris.

Mary Garden, *Mary Garden's Story* – Michal Joseph, © 1951 Simon & Schuster, Inc.

Penelope Gilliatt, *One By One* and *What's It Like Out?* – Secker & Warburg.

Elinor Glyn, *Sayings of Grandma* – Gerald Duckworth.

Virginia Graham, *Everything's Too Something* – Country Life; *Say Please* – The Harvill Press.

Barbara Hepworth, *J P Hodin* – Lund Humphries.

Hedda Hopper, *From Under Your Hat* – © 1952 by Hedda Hopper, reprinted by permission of Doubleday.

Fannie Hurst, *Anatomy of Me* – the executors of the Fannie Hurst Estate.

Margery Hurst, *No Glass Slipper* – Arlington Books.

Ann Jellicoe, *The Knack* – Faber & Faber.

Elsa Lanchester, *Charles Laughton and I* – Faber & Faber.

Caroline Lejeune, *Chestnuts in her Lap* – Phoenix House.

Belle Livingstone, *Belle Out of Order* – Wm Heinemann; Laurence Pollinger.

Anita Loos, *No Mother to Guide Her* – Arthur Barker.

Elizabeth Marbury, *My Crystal Ball* – Hutchinson.

Elsa Maxwell, *The Celebrity Circus* – W H Allen; *I Married the World* – Wm. Heinemann.

ACKNOWLEDGMENTS

Nancy Mitford, *Noblesse Oblige* – Hamish Hamilton.

Ethel Watts Mumford, *New Cynics Calendar of Revised Wisdom* – Paul Elder.

Dorothy Parker, *The Portable Dorothy Parker* and *General Review of the Sex Situation* – Viking Press and the Estate of the late Dorothy Parker.

Mary Pickford, *Sunshine and Shadow* – Wm Heinemann; Doubleday.

Mary Quant, *Quant by Quant* – Cassell.

Helena Rubinstein, *My Life for Beauty* – © 1964, 1965, 1966, Helena Rubinstein Foundation; the Bodley Head.

Helen Rowland, *Reflections of a Bachelor Girl* – Stanley Paul.

Elsa Schiaparelli, *Shocking Life* – E P Dutton; J M Dent.

Karl von Schumacher, *The du Barry* – G G Harrap.

Edith Sitwell, *English Women* – Aldus Books (Collins).

Cornelia Otis Skinner, *That's Me All Over* – Constable.

Muriel Spark, *Doctors of Philosophy* – Macmillan.

Elizabeth Sprigge, *Gertrude Stein* – Hamish Hamilton.

Han Suyin, *A Many-Splendoured Thing* – Jonathan Cape; Little Brown.

Maggie Teyte, *Star on the Door* – Putnam.

Carolyn Wells, Mary Wilson Little, Ethel Watts Mumford – *Dictionary of Humorous Quotations* – Evan Esar.

Elsie de Wolfe, *After All* – Wm Heinemann.

Virginia Woolf, *The Moment* – Hogarth Press.

And the editors of the *Evening News*, the *Evening Standard*, *The Guardian*, the *Sunday Times*, the *Sunday Express*, *The Times*, the *Daily Mail*, *The Observer*, the *Daily Mirror*, *Woman*.

We owe a special debt of gratitude to the *Daily Express* and its chief librarian Mr E W Merrett, and his staff, for their considerable help.

Index

Acton, Eliza, 128
   Famous cookery expert
Adler, Polly, 9
   One-time, 'Premier Madam' of New York
Arden, Elizabeth, 134
   Founder of a great beauty business
Arnould, Sophie, 143–4
   French opera star
Asquith, Dame Margot, 10–11, 80, 105, 119–20
   Countess of Oxford and Asquith
Astell, Mary, 80, 105–6
   Author
Astor, Lady Nancy, 12, 120
   First woman to sit in the House of Commons
Aubernon, Madame, 12–13
   French hostess known for her salon
Austen, Jane, 13, 81
   Novelist
Aylesbury, Lady, 14

Ballard, Bettina, 135
   One-time Editor of 'Vogue'
Bankhead, Tallulah, 144–5
   American stage and screen star
Bardot, Brigitte, 143, 145–6
   French screen star
Barnet, Lady Isobel, 14
   British television personality
Barry, Madame du, 93, 130–1
   Second Mistress of Louis XV

Bashkirtseff, Marie, 14, 106
   Russian artist and writer
Bedford, Duchess of, 15
   French-born wife of the present Duke
Behn, Aphra, 15, 81
   Playwright who scandalised her generation
Bellamy, Georgianna Anne, 106
   Illegitimate daughter of Lord Tyrawley
Belmont, Mrs Oliver, 81
   Queen of American high society
Bernhardt, Sarah, 146
   A legendary name in the theatre
Beyfus, Drusilla, 81
   Author and journalist
Bingham, Charlotte, 15–16
   Novelist
Bingham, Madeleine, 16, 128–9
   Writer
Blessington, Countess of, 16–19, 82
   Novelist
Bliven, Naomi, 19
   American writer
Boleyn, Anne, 19
   Second wife of Henry VIII
Bottome, Phyllis, 19
   Novelist
Boyd, Nancy, 20, 121
   Pseudonym of Edna St Vincent Millay, American writer and poet
Braddock, E M, 121
   MP known affectionately as 'Bessie'

171

INDEX

Braddon, M E, 82
Novelist
Brahms, Caryl, 147
Author, playwright, critic
Brontë, Charlotte, 21
Novelist
Brophy, Brigid, 129
Author and journalist
Browning, Elizabeth Barrett, 21
Poet
Buck, Pearl, 21-2
American novelist and Nobel Prize winner
Burton, Baroness, 121
Former Labour MP
Butler, Joyce, 122
Labour MP

Campbell, Mrs Patrick, 148
Famous actress
Caroline, Queen, 82
Wife of King George II
Carter, Ernestine, 135
Journalist
Cartland, Barbara, 83
Novelist and biographer
Catherine of Genoa, 83
Devoted her life to the sick
Catherine of Sienna, St, 106
Ascetic and visionary
Catherine the Great, 22, 93-4, 122
The famous Russian Empress
Cavendish, Margaret, 107
Duchess of Newcastle
Centlivre, Mrs, 107
Playwright
Chanel, Gabrielle 'Coco', 135-6
Doyenne of Paris fashion
Charlotte, Queen, 22
Wife of King George III
Chase, Ilka, 22-3, 83
American actress and author
Christina of Sweden, 23, 84, 108
Former Queen – nicknamed 'Queen of Sodom'
Christie, Agatha, 23-4, 136
Famous author of 'Whodunnits'

Cleopatra, 129-30
Sixth Queen of Egypt
Cleves, Anne of, 24
Fourth wife of Henry VIII
Colette, 24-5, 108
French novelist
Collins, Jackie, 148
Actress and novelist
Compton-Burnett, Dame Ivy, 70
Companion of Literature
Cooper, Dame Gladys, 71
Stage and screen star
Cooper, Lady Diana, 25
Author and Society hostess
Corelli, Marie, 84
Best selling author of romances
Cornuel, Madame, 108
Salon leader
Cowles, Fleur, 25-6
Author and journalist
Cowley, Hannah, 26
Playwright
Craster, Mrs Edmund, 26
English Poet

Dane, Clemence, 27, 84-5
Pseudonym of Winifred Ashton, playwright and novelist
Dariaux, Geneviève Antoine, 27-8, 109, 136-7
Writer and Directrice of the Paris couture house of Nina Ricci
Dartmouth, Lady, 28
Politician and hostess
Davis, Bette, 148-9
Film and stage star
Défand, Marquise du, 29, 94
Eighteenth-century salon owner and friend of Horace Walpole
Deshoulières, Madame, 29
French poet
Dickinson, Emily, 29
American poet
Dietrich, Marlene, 149
Stage and screen star
Drabble, Margaret, 30
Novelist

INDEX

Dressler, Marie, 149–50
  Screen star
Drouet, Juliette, 94–5
  Mistress of Victor Hugo
Duncan, Isadora, 150
  Eccentric actress and personality
Dunn, Nell, 30
  Playwright and novelist
Duse, Eleonora, 85, 150–1
  Famous Italian actress

Edgeworth, Maria, 30–1
  Writer
Edwards, Anne, 31, 110
  Journalist
Eliot, George, 31–2, 111
  Novelist
'Elizabeth' (Lady Russell), 32
  Novelist
Elizabeth I, Queen, 32–3, 85, 111
  The 'Virgin Queen'
Elliot, Baroness, 122
  Dame of the British Empire
Enclos, Ninon de l', 86–7
  Seventeenth-century feminist, admired by Richelieu
Esparbes, Comtesse d', 95–6
  Mistress of Louis XV
Ewing, Winifred, 123
  First Scottish Nationalist MP

Fanshawe, Lady Anne, 33
  Wife of a favourite Ambassador of Charles II
Fée, Madame, 87
  Little-known French wit
Ferber, Edna, 33
  American author and playwright
Fields, Gracie, 151–2
  International music hall entertainer
Fitzherbert, Mrs, 96
  Mistress of George IV
Fleming, Joan, 34
  Crime novelist and playwright
Floris, Maria, 131–2
  Royal cake-maker

Gaitskell, Baroness, 123
  Widow of the Labour Party Leader
Garden, Mary, 152–3
  Famous opera star
Genée-Isitt, Dame Adeline, 71
  A great name in ballet
Gilliatt, Penelope, 34–5, 112
  Author and critic
Gingold, Hermione, 153
  Comedienne and actress
Glyn, Elinor, 35, 105
  Novelist
Glynn, Prudence, 137
  Journalist
Graham, Sheilah, 112
  Journalist and writer
Graham, Virginia, 35–6, 112, 132
  Author and playwright
Green Felicity, 138
  Journalist
Grenfell, Joyce, 154
  Entertainer
Guilbert, Yvette, 87–8, 154–5
  Famous French diseuse
Guinan, Texas, 36, 88
  American night-club queen
Gwynne, Nell, 96–7
  Mistress of Charles II

Hayes, Helen, 155
  American stage and screen star
Henie, Sonja, 36
  World skating star
Hepburn, Katharine, 155
  Famous stage and screen star
Hepworth, Dame Barbara, 71
  Leading British sculptress
Heywood, Anne, 156
  Film star
Highsmith, Patricia, 37
  Popular 'Who-dunnit' author
Hopper, Hedda, 37, 112, 139
  Hollywood columnist
Horsbrugh, Baroness, 124
  Former Conservative MP
Howard, Henrietta, 97–8
  Mistress of George II

INDEX

Howe, Julia Ward, 37
Author of 'Battle Hymn of the Republic'
Hull, Josephine, 156
Actress
Hurst, Fannie, 38
Eminent American novelist
Hurst, Margery, 38-9, 113
One of Britain's leading business women
Hyde, Catherine, 39
Duchess of Queensberry

Ince, Angela, 39-40, 113
Journalist

Janis, Elsie, 156
American stage star
Jeger, Lena, 124
Labour MP
Jellicoe, Anne, 40
Playwright

Kelly, Mary, 40
Crime novelist
Kendal, Dame Madge, 72
Stage star
Kingston, Duchess of, 41
The 'Bigamous Duchess'
Kitt, Eartha, 156
International Star
Knight, Dame Laura, 72
Eminent artist

Lafayette, Madame de, 41
French author
Lamb, Lady Caroline, 41-2, 88
Novelist remembered chiefly for her liaison with Lord Byron
Lanchester, Elsa, 157
Screen and stage star
Lee, The Rt Hon Jennie, 124
Politician
Leigh, Vivien, 157-8
Stage and screen star
Lejeune, Caroline, 158-9
Author and critic

Lespinasse, Julie de, 98-9
Leading light of eighteenth-century Paris intellectuals
Lestor, Joan, 124-5
Labour MP
Lillie, Beatrice, 159-61
Star comedienne
Little, Mary Wilson, 42-3, 114, 139
American writer
Livingstone, Belle, 43-4, 99
American actress and hostess of the Edwardian era
Lloyd, Marie, 162
One of the 'greats' of the British music hall
Lombard, Carole, 162
Screen star
Loos, Anita, 44-5, 114
American novelist and playwright
Loynes, Comtesse de, 99-100
Mistress of Prince Napoleon, Dumas Fils and Flaubert
Luce, Clare Boothe, 45-6, 115
Author and playwright
Luynes, Duchesse de, 46
French aristocrat of the 1890s

McCormick, Anne O'Hare, 47
American journalist
'Madame', 47-8, 88
Duchess of Orleans
Maintenon, Marquise de, 100
Mistress, then second wife of Louis XIV
Mansfield, Jayne, 115
Screen sex symbol
Mansfield, Katherine, 48
Author
Marbury, Elizabeth, 48-9
Playwright and authors' agent
Marchesi, Blanche, 163
Famous singer and teacher
Markova, Dame Alicia, 73
Prima Ballerina assoluta
Marlborough, Duchess of, 49
Died 1744, aged 84
Mathilde, Princess, 89
Niece of Napoleon I

INDEX

Maurier, Daphne du, 49, 89
Novelist and playwright
Maxwell, Elsa, 49–51, 89, 125
Famous hostess
Melba, Dame Nellie, 73–4
Famous prima donna
Menken, Adah Isaacs, 163
Much-maligned actress
Meyer, Caren, 51
Journalist
Millay, Edna St Vincent, 52
American writer and poet
Mitford, Nancy, 52–3, 89–90
Novelist and biographer
Monroe, Marilyn, 164
Film star
Montagu, Elizabeth, 53
'Queen of the blue stockings'
More, Hannah, 55
Prolific writer
Mumford, Ethel Watts, 55–7
American novelist and humorist

Naylor, Margot, 57
Financial journalist
Necker, Madame, 57
Mother of Madame de Staël
Nightingale, Florence, 57–8
'The Lady with the Lamp' in the Crimean War

O'Brien, Edna, 58, 90
Novelist
Otero, Caroline (La Belle), 100–1
Actress and famous cocotte
'Ouida', 58, 115
Reacted against the prudery of feminine novelists of her day

Parker, Dorothy, 59
American writer
Parr, Catherine, 59–60
Sixth wife of Henry VIII
Phillips, Baroness, 125
Widow of General Secretary of Labour Party
Pickford, Mary, 164–5
America's 'sweetheart'

Pinzieux, Madame de, 90
French writer
Proops, Marjorie, 115–16
Journalist and broadcaster
Prunier, Madame, 132
Famous Anglo-French restaurateur

Quant, Mary, 139–40
Originator of a new and modern school of fashion

Rachel, Elisa Felix, 165
Great French actress
Rambert, Dame Marie, 74
Founder of famous ballet
Récamier, Madame, 101–2
Mistress of Chateaubriand
Rieux, Madame de, 102
Mistress of King Henry III of France
Robson, Dame Flora, 74
Screen and stage star
Rogers, Ginger, 165–6
Screen and stage star
Roland, Madame, 60
One of the leading figures in the French Revolution
Rowland, Helen, 60, 90–1, 116–17
American author and journalist
Rubinstein, Helena, 134, 140–1
Founder of a famous beauty house
Russell, Rosalind, 166
Stage and screen star

Sand, George, 60–1, 102–3, 117, 125
Pseudonym of Amantine Lucile Aurore Baroness Dudevant, great French writer
Sappho, 61
Greatest woman poet of Greece
Sartory, Madame de, 91
French writer
Schiaparelli, Elsa, 93, 133, 141
Founder of famous French fashion-beauty house
Scott-James, Anne, 61–2
Novelist and journalist

175

INDEX

Scudery, Madeleine de, 62, 117
French author
Sévigné, Madame de, 62, 118
French writer
Sitwell, Dame Edith, 74-5, 133, 142
Renowned poet
Skinner, Cornelia Otis, 63
American actress and writer
Spark, Muriel, 63
Novelist and playwright
Staël, Madame de, 80, 91, 103
Famous writer
Stein, Edith, 63
Religious zealot
Stein, Gertrude, 64
The most controversial writer of the century
Stocks, Baroness, 126
Author and radio personality
Stopes, Marie, 91
Protagonist of birth control
Summerskill, the Rt Hon Baroness, 126
Life peeress and former MP
Suyin, Han, 64, 92
Novelist
Sylva, Carmen, 65
Pseudonym of Elizabeth, Queen of Romania

Taylor, Elizabeth, 166
International screen star
Tempest, Dame Marie, 75
Great stage comedienne
Teresa, Empress Maria, 65
Queen of Hungary and Bohemia, wife of Holy Roman Emperor Francis I
Terry, Dame Ellen, 75-6
Actress who has become a legend
Teyte, Dame Maggie, 76
Famous opera star
Thirkell, Angela, 65
Novelist
Thorndike, Dame Sybil, 76
Eminent actress
Tindall, Gillian, 92
Novelist and journalist
Tour, Madame de la, 92
Little-known French wit
Trench, Melesina, 66
Diarist
Tucker, Sophie, 167
Last of the 'Red-hot mamas'

Valois, Marguerite de, 92
A scandalous Queen of France
Vanbrugh, Dame Irene, 77
Stage star of her era
Victoria, Queen, 127
British Queen

Wells, Carolyn, 66-7
American mistress of Parody
West, Dame Rebecca, 77, 118
Novelist and journalist
West Mae, 167
Screen and stage star
Whitehorn, Katherine, 67-8
Author and journalist
Wilkinson, Ellen, 127
Politician
Wilson, Harriette, 104
Nineteenth-century mistress of Earl of Craven and Duke of Wellington
Wolfe, Elsie de, 68-9, 142
Actress and society hostess
Woolf, Virginia, 69
Eminent writer
Wootton, Baroness, 127
Life Peeress
Wordsworth, Elizabeth, 69
Great-niece of the poet